ENDORSEMENTS

I have a deep appreciation for Teresa Liebscher and her heart to see the body of Christ set free in every area of life. Her latest book *The Book of Healing: A Journey to Inner Healing Through the Book of Job* is an incredible and vulnerable approach to the book of Job. She does a great job of helping the reader to see another part of the story that is easy to miss or overlook. My prayer is this book helps from people all over to come to a place to experience freedom in every area of their life.

ERIC JOHNSON
Bethel Church
Author & Speaker

It would be impossible to overstate how much God desires us to experience the freedom He has made available to us. One thing I have always appreciated about my mom is her desire to walk with people and help them discover that freedom for themselves. In *The Book of Healing: A Journey to Inner Healing Through the Book of Job*, she brings to light, in a story that is so many times misunderstood, profound truths that will empower people to see God more clearly and embrace a life of health. Through years of study and practical and accessible life stories, *The*

Book of Healing invites you to experience inner healing in a powerful and life-changing way.

BANNING LIEBSCHER
Pastor and Founder of Jesus Culture
Author of *Rooted: The Hidden Places
Where God Develops Us*

Teresa's book is not only a great read but a must read! For those who have been stuck in cycles of pain, Teresa's ability to connect people to the Lord shines through in her understanding of the book of Job. Teresa's message is clear—if we see Job not as a book on suffering but inner healing—we can better understand our relationships to pain and move forward in our connection with God.

DAWNA DE SILVA
Pastor, Author and Founder/Leader
of Bethel Sozo Ministry

Teresa Liebscher's book is a must read. Truthfully, I have always avoided the book Of Job. When I used my Bible and read the book of Job, I never really felt safe in my world. So when in doubt I skipped it. The revelations presented in this book allow me to see Father God and talk with Him about life in a way I have never been able to do before! If you desire a deeper connection to Father God, this is definitely the book for you. No need for me to avoid Job anymore!

DR. JEFFREY BARSCH
Author and Bethel Sozo Center Counselor

the BOOK *of* HEALING

A JOURNEY
TO INNER HEALING THROUGH
THE BOOK OF JOB

TERESA LIEBSCHER

DESTINY IMAGE® PUBLISHERS, INC.

P.O. Box 310, Shippensburg, PA 17257-0310

"Promoting Inspired Lives."

This book and all other Destiny Image and Destiny Image Fiction books are available at Christian bookstores and distributors worldwide.

Cover design by Eileen Rockwell
Interior design by Terry Clifton

For more information on foreign distributors, call 717-532-3040.

Reach us on the Internet: www.destinyimage.com.

ISBN 13 TP: 978-0-7684-1857-6
ISBN 13 eBook: 978-0-7684-1858-3
ISBN 13 HC: 978-0-7684-1860-6
ISBN 13 LP: 978-0-7684-1859-0

For Worldwide Distribution, Printed in the U.S.A.
1 2 3 4 5 6 7 8 / 22 21 20 19 18

Acknowledgments

THIS BOOK WOULD NOT HAVE HAPPENED IF IT WAS not for the following people:

Katy who helped turn my world into the written word,

Darrell C whose questions guided me,

Dawna who provides the atmosphere to practice my "gifting,"

Cory who worked his fingers to the bone to put words to paper,

All those friends who keep encouraging me through my doubts.

Thanks Destiny Image for opening up a new world for me.

Remember that you have made me like clay;
and will you return me to the dust?
Did you not pour me out like milk
and curdle me like cheese?
You clothed me with skin and flesh,
and knit me together with bones and sinews.
You have granted me life and steadfast love,
and your care has preserved my spirit.
—JOB 10:9-12 ESV

Author's Note

Each story in this book represents a true story from a client followed by My Story. I have changed the names of clients to protect their identity.

CONTENTS

FOREWORD

I MET TERESA LIEBSCHER OVER TWENTY YEARS ago. Little did I know that today we would be leading a worldwide inner-healing ministry bringing breakthrough to thousands across the globe. I have always felt Teresa had an important message on healing, so it excited me to finally get my hands on her manuscript.

Teresa has one of the most powerful personal stories of deliverance I have ever heard. Coming from years of abuse and trauma, she is a radical testimony to what can be achieved when stewarding an honest relationship with God.

Stewarding this honesty is what *The Book of Healing: A Journey to Inner Healing Through the Book of Job* is all about. Teresa finds wisdom and insight in Job's story that many have failed to grasp entirely. Examining the story through an inner-healing lens, she puts forth the argument that the book of Job is not just about human suffering, but how processing suffering with God gained Job his breakthrough.

Books on inner-healing are common. Each fills a vital role. But this one brings intimacy with God (specifically friendship) to a new level. Speaking in a conversational tone, Teresa brings her readers on a journey—one that connects them to the Father—and seeks to help anchor Christians in seasons that may not feel safe.

Everyone has struggled through storms. Sometimes the greatest lesson is learning how to stand above them. Jesus demonstrated this in His dealing with the disciples. When everyone else was panicked, Jesus rested in the hold of the ship—fast asleep. It was only until the disciples woke Him and asked, *"Teacher, do you not care that we are perishing?"* that Jesus rose and commanded the storm, *"Peace! Be still!"* (see Mark 4:38-39).

Pastor Bill Johnson says that you will only have authority over the storms you can sleep through. Peace has to dwell first inside of our hearts in order to seep out to effect the world around us. Teresa shows us that an aspect of gaining inner peace is stewarding an honest relationship with God where any and all pain can be processed.

I appreciate Teresa's willingness to dig deep into Job's story and walk us through key moments before, during, and after his crisis. It allows us (the reader) to be on the journey ourselves—watching Job process his fears while combatting his friends' unhelpful advice.

If you've ever felt confused, mystified, or fearful about the book of Job, then consider Teresa's insight as a safe and practical way to explore its hidden secrets. Teresa's choice to use the *Message* translation puts the ancient dialect into contemporary English. The effect is both refreshing and illuminating. Passages that may have seemed dense or "too poetic" suddenly feel transparent and lucid.

I encourage you, whether you are on your own journey of inner-healing or not, to pick up a copy of this book. Allow it to inspire you to seek a closer and more personal relationship with the Lord. Without a close connection to the Father, Son, and Holy Spirit, there is no way we can stand against life's storms and command them to "be still."

Teresa has a masterpiece with *The Book of Healing: A Journey to Inner Healing Through the Book of Job*—one that could equip a generation to succeed where others have failed. I hope you enjoy it as you begin the journey of a lifetime.

Dawna De Silva
Co-founder of Bethel Sozo, Bethel
Church, Redding, California
Author, *Sozo: Saved, Healed, and Delivered* and
Shifting Atmospheres

Prologue

Trey searched the landscape. Tents and trees loomed ahead. He could see columns of colorfully dressed men and women leading camels and livestock. Up ahead, a tent of turquoise and purple colors swirled in the breeze.

Trey looked to his master, eyes calm and serious. He hadn't spoken much since the beginning of this journey weeks before.

Clay pots rattled beside Trey as he rode atop the oxen-pulled cart. One of the servant boys behind him whispered, "Where are we?"

"Job's country," another said.

Job, Trey thought. I've heard that name before.

"Trey," A voice called from the front.

Trey looked up to see who was speaking. It was his master, frowning, "Keep moving."

"Yes, master."

Trey snapped at his reins. The oxen roared and continued forward. Behind him, the servant boys continued talking.

"I heard raiders invaded Job's fields and stole his animals."

"I heard an earthquake killed his children."

"Why are we riding out here all this way?"

The voices diminished as they rode into camp. A larger tent stood distant from the rest. Beside it were the encampments of two smaller companies with their own sets of servants and animals.

Trey pulled at his reins, and the oxen slowed. Behind him, servants descended from their mounts and unpacked.

The camp around them seemed strange and quiet. What men he did see appeared distant and silent, the women and children frightened.

One of the servant boys pointed to a distant tent.

"That must be Job's."

Trey's master descended his camel, "Set up camp."

As Trey and the others gathered supplies, their master marched hurriedly away. He was heading toward Job's tent.

"What's going on?" Trey asked.

"Who knows?" A servant boy said, bringing down a crate. "Perhaps we'll find out tomorrow."

Trey and the others did find out, but it wasn't until days later. One of the camp's guards told them Job and three men, their master among them, were sitting in silence. Each had torn their robes and were covered in dust.

The next day, Trey snuck off toward the tent. He wanted to see what his master was doing. The voices of his fellow servant boys grew quiet in the distance. Finally, he made it to Job's tent and peeked in.

INTRODUCTION

A S A LEADER OF AN INTERNATIONAL INNER-HEALING ministry, I deal with many people who struggle to connect with God. They either feel stuck, lost, or hopeless. Many of these people believe lies about themselves or suffer long-held wounds from childhood. These individuals seek wholeness, healing, and normalcy. They want the path that builds and strengthens their connections with the Lord.

I wrote this book to help believers in their pursuit of Father God, the Son Jesus, and the Holy Spirit. Studying Job, I found some information for doing this.

The Book of Healing: A Journey to Inner Healing Through the Book of Job grew out of my attempts to see Job in a new light. I am not a poetry person, so Job was always a difficult book to read. Then one day, my son gave me a copy of the Message Bible—the text translated into modern speech—and it made a huge difference!

Examining Job, I realized how familiar its characters' struggles felt. In many ways, their thoughts and struggles mirrored those of my clients. Even the advice from Job's friends resembled the words my clients and I had experienced from friends and family members.

These revelations got me thinking—what if Job was more than just a book on human suffering? Its contents certainly dealt with the issue, but what if there were secrets inside that could bring us closer in our relationships with God?

The book of Job depicts painful circumstances and discusses the options we have for understanding it. It fails, however, to truly bring an obvious answer in how to rationalize pain's existence. Perhaps this is why Job is such a frustrating book for some readers. In all the talk about why human suffering exists, neither Job, his friends, nor even God provides an answer.

Many search Job for an explanation on human suffering—but maybe that's not the point of the book. This got me thinking: if explaining the reasons for hardship is not discussed in the book, then why was it written? Reading the story, we see it begins in heaven, then follows Job as he searches for answers, then goes to him debating his friends as they try to convince him of his sin. The story ends when God appears to present a different viewpoint.

The book begins with God's interaction with satan in heaven and ends with Job encountering the Lord and acknowledging who He is. In-between this transformation is a busy section of theology—mostly carried out by Job's friends.

Once Job goes through his journey of discovery, he repents for living on "limited knowledge" of God and receives inner healing (see Job 42:6). His friends learn a lesson of who God is and Job receives more from God than he ever lost.

I could go on dissecting the story, but that would infringe on the future sections of this book. I do not wish to stir up a theological debate, but I do hope to inspire you to think differently. Perhaps Job is just a book on suffering to you, and that's fine, but maybe there is more. Possibly, by the end of this book, you will see Job as a lesson on inner healing. At the very least, I hope to encourage you to rethink a very familiar story and to see if its pages inspire you to seek a closer relationship with the Lord.

Preface

GETTING STARTED

JOB HAS A LONG HISTORY OF SCHOLARLY ANALYSIS, so this will be far from the last book written on the subject. Many influential minds have poured over its pages, including the great Saint Augustine, Thomas Aquinas, Martin Luther, and C.S. Lewis.

In scholarly circles, the book is considered a classic of world literature. Categorized as a piece of wisdom literature, it presents the all-important question, "Why, in a world over which God has jurisdiction, do innocent people suffer?"[1]

Rabbinic tradition indicates the author could be Moses, but this is at best an educated guess. We have no idea on the date of its origin, but theologians argue it is one of the oldest books in the Bible.

Regardless of how readers see its development, Job remains one of the most highly regarded pieces of writing in human history. The manner in which this book is written is handled by providing the information in a poetic storytelling form.

To begin our examination, let's look where it all begins—the prologue.

PROLOGUE

Every great story has a beginning, and Job's story begins in the prologue. It consists of the first two chapters and establishes Job as a man of character. Right off, we see Job as a righteous man devoted to God and family. He even takes extra steps (in the form of burnt offerings) to please the Lord:

> *There was a man in the land of Uz whose name was Job, and that man was blameless and upright, one who feared God and turned away from evil. There were born to him seven sons and three daughters...And when the days of the feast had run their course, Job would send and consecrate them, and he would rise early in the morning and offer burnt offerings according to the number of them all. For Job said, "It may be that my children have sinned, and cursed*

God in their hearts." Thus Job did continually (Job 1:1-2,5 ESV).

We see that Job is so devoted to his family that he rises up early each morning to offer prayers for his children. He does this so that when his sons and daughters attend parties, they will remain covered. Job doesn't even know if his children *do* sin, but he offers sacrifices to God anyway "just in case."

In the prologue, we also get a glimpse of Job's wealth. The Bible says, *"He possessed 7,000 sheep, 3,000 camels, 500 yoke of oxen, 500 female donkeys, and very many servants"* (Job 1:3 ESV). The author goes on to say that Job was *"the greatest of all the people of the east"* (Job 1:3 ESV).

We have no way of knowing how wealthy Job was, but we can assume he was doing quite well. I can imagine he had hundreds, if not thousands, of workers. And I'm not sure what the architecture of his time resembled, but I can imagine it looked pretty fancy.

In the following scene, we transition to heaven. Angels enter the Lord's presence, and satan follows the angels, *"The Lord said to Satan, 'From where have you come?' Satan answered the Lord and said, 'From going to and fro on the earth, and from walking up and down on it'"* (Job 1:7 ESV).

The next part of the story is interesting to me. It seems, almost out of the blue, that God brings up Job's character. He says, *"Have you [satan] considered my servant Job, that there is none like him on the earth, a blameless and upright man, who fears God and turns away from evil?"* (Job 1:8 ESV).

God's "bragging" about Job's character prompts an interesting response from satan. He questions Job's righteousness by asking,

> *Does Job fear God for no reason? Have you not put a hedge around him and his house and all that he has, on every side? You have blessed the work of his hands, and his possessions have increased in the land. But stretch out your hand and touch all that he has, and he will curse you to your face* (Job 1:9-11).

Satan indicates to God that, "Of course Job is righteous...look how well You've blessed him! But what if all his blessing was taken away? How righteous would he be then?" Satan presents a challenge to God's declaration, "You say that Job is faithful? Then let me test him."

At this point, I'm not sure why God gives satan permission. Regardless of what I think about all this, God allows satan to attack Job's possessions. His only limitation is to avoid destroying Job's health.

In the next verses, we see Job's children killed, his livestock stolen, and most of his servants murdered. Yet even after all these trials, Job remains humble and refuses to curse God. Job says, *"Naked I came from my mother's womb, and naked I'll return to the womb of the earth. God gives, God takes. God's name be ever blessed"* (Job 1:21).

Job's reaction in the midst of these trials (not blaming God and choosing to hold onto his integrity) sets the stage for the second confrontation in heaven. The angels return to God and—lo and behold—the accuser is with them. God says,

> *Have you considered my servant Job, that there is none like him on the earth, a blameless and upright man, who fears God and turns away from evil? He still holds fast his integrity, although you incited me against him to destroy him without reason* (Job 2:3 ESV).

He identifies the devil's attempt to "trick" Him into destroying his servant and basically says, "You tried, bud, but failed."

The devil refuses to give up. In his mind, he still has one more card to play. The devil claims, *"All that a man has he will give for his life. But stretch out your hand and touch his bone and his flesh, and he will curse you to your face"* (Job 2:4-5 ESV).

Most of us know the rest of the story: God gives satan permission to attack Job's health, and his body breaks out in horrendous boils. Hearing of all the tragedies that have occurred, Job's friends—Eliphaz, Bildad, and Zophar—travel far from their homes to provide comfort, insight, and companionship.

SYMPOSIUM

The second and largest part of the story centers on Job and his three friends. Scholarly articles call this section the *symposium*, which means "a collection of opinions or intellectual arguments expressed by several persons on a given subject."[2]

The intellectual arguments are carried out by Job's friends: Eliphaz, Bildad, and Zophar. Throughout this section, we see them try to explain Job's suffering through religious logic.

Eliphaz's name means "God of gold" and interestingly has ties with Esau (Jacob's brother who settled in Teman).[3] Bildad, whose name has an uncertain origin, translates as "confusing love."[4] Zophar, finally, is defined as "sparrow" or "depart early."[5] Both Bildad's and Zophar's ethnicities are mentioned only in the book of Job.

Job's friends try to use their knowledge to provide reason and helpful arguments. According to them, Job is a sinner who *must* repent, and only when he does so will his tragedies be resolved:

> *Think! Has a truly innocent person ever ended*
> *up on the scrap heap?*
> *Do genuinely upright people ever lose out in the*
> *end?*
> *It's my observation that those who plow evil...*
> *reap evil...*
> (Job 4:7-8).

This sentiment of *those who reap evil, sow evil* presents itself largely throughout the friends' discourse. Job's resistance to their ideas is his belief that he has not sinned, but God, for some reason, has betrayed him:

> *Job says, "I am innocent, but God denies me*
> *justice"* (Job 34:5 NIV).

The main conflict in this section is that Job refuses to agree with any of his friends' arguments. It's like an endless game of tennis with each companion sending over a volley of statements only to have them batted away with ferocity.

Each of Job's friends sounds theologically correct, but none of them seem very helpful. Job's response shows us just how much he dislikes their opinions:

I've had all I can take of your talk. What a
bunch of miserable comforters!
Is there no end to your windbag speeches? What's
your problem that you go on and on like this?
(Job 16:2-3).

According to Eliphaz, Bildad, and Zophar, if Job only realizes he is the problem and confesses his sin, then God will appear and heal all the trials that have occurred.

ELIHU'S APPEARANCE

The third and possibly most elusive section of the book (besides the Lord's) involves that of Elihu. At the end of the symposium, after each of Job's friends has had their say, a young man, Elihu, appears. His name translates as "He is my God," and he argues with such intensity that Job nor any of his friends have time to interrupt.[6] In fact, the young man only quiets when God bursts onto the scene.

Not much is known about Elihu, where he is from, or what happens after he speaks. Some scholars debate whether he is the true author of the story. This is yet another unsolved theory. All we get is his name, age, and energetic personality which seems to be hurrying to get everything out before being silenced.

NATURE POEMS AND EPILOGUE

The fourth section is known as the "Nature Poems" and is when God finally intervenes. Using pictures and metaphors from the natural world, God paints the immensity of the universe and challenges Job for even thinking he could begin to understand His ways.

The epilogue, of course, is where Job's fate is decided. I am purposely leaving these later sections vague because we will go into them in depth later. For now, I want you to be aware of the overall sections of the story and see what each one roughly contains.

THE JOURNEY BEGINS

The majority of this book will focus on the nitty-gritty of Job's conversations with his friends and, finally, the Lord. I use the term "rounds" instead of chapters because I want to capture the sequential feel of the book. Rounds one through three cover the entire discourse between Job and his friends. Round four covers Elihu's discourse directed at Job and his friends. Round five, finally, deals with God's conversation with Job, and the latter's acknowledgment of his shortcomings and the result of this admission.

Hopefully, you will gain some insight into how Job processed his pain and see how his honesty—not theological eloquence—brought peace from God. Without further delay, let's begin.

NOTES

1. "Summary and Analysis Job," *CliffsNotes*, https://www.cliffsnotes.com/literature/o/old-testament -of-the-bible/summary-and-analysis/job.

2. Dictionary.com, s.v. "Symposium," accessed January 8, 2018, http://www.dictionary.com/browse/symposium.

3. Lexicon: Strong's H464 – *'Eliyphaz*, s.v. "Eliphaz," Blue Letter Bible, accessed January 10, 2018, https://www.blueletterbible.org/lang/lexicon/lexicon.cfm?Strongs=H464&t=ESV.

4. Lexicon: Strong's H1085 – *Bildad*, s.v. "Bildad," Blue Letter Bible, accessed January 10, 2018, https://www.blueletterbible.org/lang/lexicon/lexicon.cfm?Strongs=H1085&t=ESV.

5. Lexicon: Strong's H6691 – *Tsowphar*, s.v. "Zophar," Blue Letter Bible, accessed January 10, 2018, https://www.blueletterbible.org/lang/lexicon/lexicon.cfm?Strongs=H6691&t=ESV.

6. Lexicon: Strong's H453 – *'Eliyhuw*, s.v. "Elihu," Blue Letter Bible, accessed January 10, 2018, https://www.blueletterbible.org/lang/lexicon/lexicon.cfm?Strongs=H453&t=ESV.

Round One

SHATTERED REPOSE

*My repose is shattered, my peace destroyed. No
rest for me, ever—death has invaded life.*
—JOB 3:26

Trey lifted the tent corner and peeked inside.

Four men sat in the inner area, the most hideous of
them in the center.

Almost naked, he lifted a piece of pottery from the
floor and scraped at a huge boil on his side.

Trey held his breath. He had never seen a person
so grotesque.

One of the men beside Job wept. It was Trey's master, Eliphaz! Trey barely recognized him. He sat on
torn garments, beard scraggly, scalp covered in ash.

Trey's master lifted his head to speak, but hesitated and returned his gaze to the floor. The others on either side of him sat in silence with similar looks of pain.

Trey crept back out from the tent and lowered its corner. He had never seen so much misery in one place. As he tiptoed away, a voice croaked from within. It sounded like his master, Eliphaz.

Trey scurried back to the tent and peeked in. Sure enough, it was his master speaking.

MISERABLE HEARTACHE

Joyce and I talked for some time in my office. She had blindly made an appointment with me weeks before not understanding how I could be helpful. She had tried several different healing methods over the years: prayer lines, healing rooms, counseling, and other ministries. After each attempt, she would experience some measure of peace but then crash and burn weeks later.

I noticed Joyce's hair seemed stringy and oily in our session. Her clothes did not match, and she looked unkempt. As she avoided my eyes, her hands fluttered in constant motion.

I listened to Joyce discuss what had occurred in her past and noticed a pattern. Every time she left a meeting, she felt hopeful; but as the days passed, discouragement grew.

In Joyce's case, an unfortunate call from her senior pastor sent her into a depressive spiral. During this conversation, the pastor informed her that she had been taken off the ministry team. His reasoning was that some of the leaders felt Joyce needed to receive more inner healing before being trusted to minister to other people. This information hurt because Joyce thought she was getting better. Now there seemed no end to her miserable heartache.

After a short pause, Joyce blurted out, "I wish I had never been born."

Startled, I asked, "Why?"

"My parents never wanted me anyway. If I was never born, my problems would be over because they would never have started."

"That's an interesting assumption," I said. "Why don't we ask Father God what He thinks about that?"

A PROMISE OF PEACE

This type of statement might seem out of place, but you'd be surprised at how many Christians struggle with this thought. Losing life for the sake of comfort is not something new, but being able to deal with life's circumstances in a healthy manner is key.

Finding peace and applying it to our situations is God's way of living, but sometimes it feels easier said than done. Jesus warned that we might not always have circumstances the way we want them, but at least we have Him whenever necessary:

Peace I leave with you; my peace I give you. I do not give to you as the world gives. Do not let your hearts be troubled and do not be afraid (John 14:27 NIV).

I have told you these things, so that in me you may have peace. In this world you will have trouble. But take heart! I have overcome the world (John 16:33 NIV).

By allowing peace to flow from Him, Jesus gave us an option when dealing with pain. Evangelist, Billy Graham, speaks to this phenomenon:

The sea was beating against the rocks in huge, dashing waves. The lightning was flashing, the thunder roaring, the wind was blowing; but the little bird was asleep in the crevice of the rock, its head serenely under its wing, sound asleep. That is peace—to be able to sleep in the storm! In Christ, we are relaxed and at peace in the midst of the confusions, bewilderments, and perplexities of this life.

> The storm rages, but our hearts are at rest. We
> have found peace—at last![1]

"The little bird asleep in the crevice of the rock..." this
is the peace we hope for that is available. The Bible promises us access to this peace, but those who struggle to take
hold of it think, *God, I can't deal with this pain. It's too
much!* In other cases, people succumb to lies like, *I can't
live like this. I'd rather be in dead.*

As the co-leader of an international inner healing ministry, I hear hundreds of Christians voice
this sentiment.

A WAY OUT

In Matthew 14, Jesus admonished His disciples for
their lack of peace during the storm. After witnessing a
miracle of food multiplication, they saw Jesus crossing
the lake and assumed He was a ghost! These are exam-
ples of how the enemy can steal our peace by focusing on
circumstances rather than God's perspective.

People use many options to find lasting peace. Some
use drugs, addictions, or suicide. These are just some of
the worldly options Christians are taught to avoid. A
more common choice for Christians is to wish they had
never been born.

People usually don't come to my office until they have encountered this hopeless state. Many are not aware that their problems are spiritual, and spiritual issues cannot be fixed by simply wishing them away. As a last resort, they schedule an inner healing session and hope the "ministry person" will be able to hear what God has to say so they can transfer His wisdom into their spiritual bank accounts.

People who usually come to me have typically heard through positive word of mouth and hope I will pray with them and discover their spiritual slipups so they can be healed. Many of them are desperate—willing to do anything.

JOB'S STORY

Keeping this desperation in mind, let us return to Job's story. In the prologue, we see Job's livestock stolen, his children killed, and many of his servants slaughtered. According to any human being's perception, Job seems to be having a pretty bad day.

As word spreads of Job's tragedy, three of his friends— Eliphaz, Bildad, and Zophar—leave their countries to come to his aide. I assume these are pretty close friends because people don't tend to travel long distances to visit strangers.

We don't know how far each traveled or how long they stayed with Job. What the Bible does tell us is Job was covered in sores, so much so that he was barely recognizable. His friends tore their robes in misery and wept, even sitting together for days without speaking. So far, Job's friends seem pretty reliable, or at least deeply sympathetic.

As I read this passage in the Message translation, several questions came to mind: are Job and his friends sitting in the midst of an assembly? Or are they outside by themselves? Are they in private quarters? Or are they sitting in the midst of camp? When Job finally begins his speech, who and what is around him?

It is important to remember that Job is one of the wealthiest people in all the land. We can assume he has a vast number of people living in his dominion. Most likely, there are many tents around his area with people milling about, living their lives by cooking, cleaning, and watching children.

In this setting, we find a man responding in much the same way as many would today—angry, upset, and confused! His first words are similar to many discouraged clients who weep in my office (but more poetic, of course):

> *Obliterate the day I was born.*
> *Blank out the night I was conceived!*

Let it be a black hole in space.
May God above forget it ever happened.
Erase it from the books...
And why? Because it released me from my
mother's womb
into a life with so much trouble
(Job 3:3-4,10).

Right out of the gate, Job begs for his name to be erased from heaven. Why? Because if he hadn't been born, he wouldn't be experiencing these problems.

As I mentioned before, many Christians who suffer severe issues struggle with these same thoughts. They find themselves voicing Job's cry: "Why is everything so hard? I wish I had never been born!"

Following this train of thought, Job stumbles onto another kernel. If life is so miserable, what is the point of even living out its existence?

What's the point of life when it doesn't make
sense,
when God blocks all the roads to meaning?
(Job 3:23).

It's easy to forget God's promises when we are facing difficulty. We humans tend to desire a way out and try anything to resolve the issue. Like Job, we wonder what the purpose of life is, and when we don't find one, decide its entire existence is reserved for pain.

At times, a friend's words of comfort can help us navigate discouragement. In other cases, they can lead us from the truth. Just as Job had friends surrounding him in difficulty, so do we tend to have companions come to our aid. Unfortunately for Job, his friends are not that helpful. They may sound logical, but their outlook of God is defined by their *own knowledge* and fails to bring any adequate answers to the table.

DOESN'T GOD USE PAIN TO "FIX" US?

One thread Job's friends try to push is the idea that God works "all things together for good." While this statement is true, people on the receiving end of tragedy rarely ever want to hear it:

> *So, what a blessing when God steps in and corrects you!*
> *Mind you, don't despise the discipline of Almighty God!*
> *True, he wounds, but he also dresses the wound; the same hand that hurts you, heals you*
> (Job 5:17-18).

Eliphaz basically states that Job should be grateful because God is using this time of crisis to correct him. Job may be suffering, but at least God is using it for his benefit.

Meanwhile, back in my office, Joyce explains how some of her friends have said the same thing. They claim that God has allowed problems in her life so she can be aware of her issues, repent, and become whole. But when Joyce repents, she still feels condemned. Unsure of what to do, she dives deeper into the mire of self-analysis.

Self-analysis is exactly what Eliphaz wants Job to do. If he can get Job to reflect on and admit his sin, then maybe God will have mercy and restore his fortunes:

> *Think! Has a truly innocent person ever ended*
> *up on the scrap heap?*
> *Do genuinely upright people ever lose out in the*
> *end?*
> *It's my observation that those who plow evil*
> *and sow trouble reap evil and trouble.*
> *One breath from God and they fall apart,*
> *one blast of his anger and there's nothing left*
> *of them*
> (Job 4:7-9).

Eliphaz's words suggest it is impossible for Job to be in the right. God is just; therefore, why would He punish an innocent person? Eliphaz sees this as an opportunity for Job to repent and be thankful, since, after all, the Lord is "improving" him.

Contrary to Eliphaz's assertion, Job is not feeling thankful at all. At the moment, there is not a thankful bone in his body. All Job feels is hurt, scared, and betrayed. He lets his friends know just how depressed he is. Not only has everything he loved been torn from him but the one relationship he could depend on—the Lord—has vanished:

> *The arrows of God Almighty are in me,*
> *poison arrows—and I'm poisoned all through!*
> *God has dumped the whole works on me*
> (Job 6:4).

In this passage, we see that Job feels sick. The idea of believing God has allowed all this to happen weighs on him so heavily that he cannot pry himself from the pit. He feels God has dumped all this tragedy on him, but *why?*

Back in my office, Joyce begs me to find the root of her problem and asks why God hasn't provided a way out. Like so many others experiencing tragedy, she wonders why God has placed her on this unfair path. Maybe God created her in a non-personal way? Maybe He is indifferent to suffering? Maybe God left her to fend for herself?

Human life is a struggle, isn't it?
It's a life sentence to hard labor.
Like field hands longing for quitting time
and working stiffs with nothing to hope for but
payday,
I'm given a life that meanders and goes
nowhere—
months of aimlessness, nights of misery!
(Job 7:1-3).

IT'S ALL "PIOUS BLUSTER!"

Eliphaz continues his argument with Job but is quickly interrupted. At this point, Job feels the advice is useless. He still doesn't have any reasons for why all this happened. He continues to seek the truth, and refuses to give in to his friend's *hot air*:

When desperate people give up on God Almighty,
their friends, at least, should stick with them.
But my brothers are fickle as a gulch in the
desert—
one day they're gushing with water
from melting ice and snow cascading out of the
mountains,
but by midsummer they're dry, gullies baked
dry in the sun
(Job 6:14-17).

There is a hint of anger in Job's voice. I can imagine, like Joyce, that he feels angry because his friends aren't providing anything helpful:

Confront me with the truth and I'll shut up,
show me where I've gone off the track.
Honest words never hurt anyone,
but what's the point of all this pious bluster?
(Job 6:24-25).

Job realizes his friends' guidance is harmful and concludes the words are untrue. He doesn't have any answers and is still not sure why such bad things have happened, but at least he can separate their poison from his truth.

Still unable to connect with God, Job decides that life is hopeless. He knows God is responsible because He created all things, but perhaps God doesn't take care of His creation:

What are mortals anyway, that you bother with them,
that you even give them the time of day?
That you check up on them every morning,
looking in on them to see how they're doing?
Let up on me, will you?
Can't you even let me spit in peace?
Even supposed I'd sinned—how would that hurt you?

You're responsible for every human being
(Job 7:17-20).

At this point, Job sinks deeper into discouragement. He knows there is a God, but perhaps He's not that interested in caring for humans.

BAD THINGS ONLY HAPPEN TO BAD PEOPLE

In the world of storytelling, we expect the good guys to win and the bad guys to lose. We enjoy it when stories end happily and feel cheated when the bad guys win. Some people dreamily expect life to follow this model, but as anyone with experience knows, sometimes life doesn't go according to plan.

The lie that "bad things only happen to bad people" is an ancient one. Seen in the book of Job, we see Eliphaz, Bildad, and Zophar try to teach their friend about this concept. They don't entertain the possibility that Job is a good person who has experienced tragedy due to circumstances beyond his control. Instead, they try to ram *their truths* down *his throat*.

The next friend to speak is Bildad, and he has some insight to share. In his mind, God is not the cause of his pain. God is good, and Job's experience is bad; therefore,

36

what Job is going through must be connected to something bad *he* has done:

> *Does God mess up?*
> *Does God Almighty ever get things backward?*
> *It's plain that your children sinned against him—*
> *otherwise, why would God have punished them?*
> *Here's what you must do—and don't put it off any longer:*
> *get down on your knees before God Almighty.*
> *If you're as innocent and upright as you say,*
> *it's not too late—he'll come running;*
> *he'll set everything right again, reestablish your fortunes.*
> *Even though you're not much right now, you'll end up better than ever*
> (Job 8:3-7).

Bildad's counsel starts right where Eliphaz's left off. He essentially states, "None of this is God's fault because He is good. It has to be yours."

Joyce's friends make similar claims. She hears the voice of condemnation as many see her as a *bad person*. Joyce tries to pray, but all it leads to is her feeling judged. After each attempt at prayer, she feels guilty. Turning to me, she hopes for healing.

Job confronts Bildad and says he has not helped or changed anything. Instead, he waits for God's answer and opens his heart to correction:

> So what's new? I know all this.
> The question is, "How can mere mortals get right with God?"
> If we wanted to bring our case before him,
> what chance would we have? Not one in a thousand...
> So how could I ever argue with him,
> construct a defense that would influence God?
> Even though I'm innocent I could never prove it;
> I can only throw myself on the Judge's mercy.
> If I called on God and he himself answered me,
> then, and only then, would I believe that he's heard me
> (Job 9:2-3, 14-16).

Job says that even if he tried to approach God, his case would be unheard. We might agree with Job's sentiment at this time and feel that even if he did go to the Lord for justice, nothing would change.

GOING TO GOD DIRECTLY

At this point, life for Job is pretty horrible. The pain he feels (compounded by the poor advice) is not helping. He feels judged by everyone around him.

In our lives, we might recognize times where we felt like we couldn't connect to the Lord. Or perhaps we struggled with family or friends who made matters worse even when they didn't mean to. Sometimes we can be in a vulnerable place and hear something hurtful that our friends and family didn't mean. Whatever the case, Job remains a very identifiable figure because, in many ways, he represents us in our deepest, darkest moments.

In the depth of his misery, Job voices his frustration at hearing condemnation from his friends:

> *Even if I say, "I'll put all this behind me,*
> *I'll look on the bright side and force a smile,"*
> *All these troubles would still be like grit in my gut*
> *since it's clear you're not going to let up.*
> *The verdict has already been handed down—"Guilty"—*
> *so what's the use of protests or appeals?*
> (Job 9:27-29).

Job continues his dialogue and gives an account of his innocence. He eventually decides the only option is to talk with God directly. He lets out all his frustration and begins to speak honestly:

> So what's this all about, anyway—this compulsion
> to dig up some dirt, to find some skeleton in my closet?
> You know good and well I'm not guilty.
> You also know no one can help me
> (Job 10:6-7).

Job's decision to talk with God is a major step towards his breakthrough. Like with any situation, hearing God's perspective can shed a glimpse into the overall circumstances. Like Joyce, Job has endured honest, yet painful, discussions with his family and friends. He now hopes to gain an audience with the Lord.

Job's friend, Zophar, decides that Job has gone too far and tries to put a stop to it. He believes that no one can come to a complete revelation of God, therefore, why try to understand His ways?

> What a flood of words! Shouldn't we put a stop to it?
> Should this kind of loose talk be permitted?
> Job, do you think you can carry on like this and we'll say nothing?
> That we'll let you rail and mock and not step in...

*Do you think you can explain the mystery of
God?*
Do you think you can diagram God Almighty?
(Job 11:2-3,7).

Zophar condemns Job's pleas to speak with God
directly. In Zophar's mind, it's foolishness to assume
someone could question God and speak with Him in a
direct way.

Despite this conversation, Job maintains his faith
and continues to desire a connection with God:

*I'm taking my case straight to God Almighty;
I've had it with you—I'm going directly to
God...
Your wise sayings are knickknack wisdom,
good for nothing but gathering dust*
(Job 13:3,12).

At this point, Job begins a conversation with God. He
pleads for understanding and asks the Lord for an explanation on the massive attack that has afflicted his life:

*Please, God, I have two requests;
grant them so I'll know I count with you:
First, lay off the afflictions;
the terror is too much for me.
Second, address me directly so I can answer you,*

or let me speak and then you answer me.
How many sins have been charged against me?
Show me the list—how bad is it?
Why do you stay hidden and silent?
Why treat me like I'm your enemy?
Why kick me around like an old tin can?
Why beat a dead horse?
You compile a long list of mean things about me,
even hold me accountable for the sins of my youth.
You hobble me so I can't move about.
You watch every move I make,
and brand me as a dangerous character.
Like something rotten, human life fast decomposes,
like a moth-eaten shirt or a mildewed blouse
(Job 13:20-28).

All of Job's pent-up frustrations come out in the open. In his mind, he's endured unfair circumstances. On top of this, his family and friends are not helping. Instead, everything they say contrasts what he believes.

Job's friends continue to argue that he must be a sinner, but Job knows he is not a bad person despite the fact that bad things are happening to him. Ultimately, he is bewildered. Hope cannot be found in them or their explanations, so he turns to the only Person he knows will have answers—God.

JOYCE'S STORY

Back in my office, I asked Joyce, "Where do you sense or feel Father God?"

"Outside," she said. "In the hallway."

"Okay." I said, then asked, "What's the expression on His face?"

She looked at me with surprise and said, "He's not angry. I expected Him to be mad because, well, I just figured He'd be disappointed."

"Let's ask Father God some questions. Is that okay?"

Hesitating, Joyce said, "Yes."

"First question. Does Father God believe the same way about you not wanting to be born?"

After repeating the prayer, Joyce shook her head, "No."

"Okay. What does Father God think about it?"

Joyce repeated the prayer, then said, "He doesn't agree with it because He created me. He wants me to be alive."

"What else is He saying?"

"He says it hurts Him to see me in pain. He wants me to know that He loves me and wants to be in a relationship with me."

Joyce broke down in tears, allowing Father God to hold her and rock her in His arms.

Once she finished crying, Joyce looked at me with a peaceful expression.

Allowing her time for the process to sink in, I waited a few moments, then asked, "The thought that you had about not being born, where is it now?"

"It's gone." She said.

"How does that make you feel?"

"Hopeful." She wipes her tear-streaming eyes. "I'm excited to start a new journey with God and see what life could be like."

The session ended soon after this with Joyce leaving my office smiling and excited for life. After encountering the Lord in just a few moments, she stepped into a whole new world of healing.

MY STORY

I too remember a time when I said and felt what Job and Joyce were expressing. I was having similar thoughts of "Where's God?" and "Why is all this happening?" My childhood was one where I learned that life was not very safe—and it was better not to be around when adults were present. In truth, I actually remember very little about my childhood.

As I became an adult, I began searching for the "normal" life. Venturing down this path, I discovered Christianity. In the churches I attended, leaders shared their interpretations of how to best live redeemed lives. This included going to church almost every day; being involved in activities the pastors suggested; and doing my best to be a religious woman, wife, and mother who could stay home and provide a stress-free environment for the kids.

I tried to be my best self—an experience I thought that was indicated in the Bible. Yet I knew my experience, which was full of fear, anger, and frustration, was not like everybody else's. I didn't know how to do life other than what I already knew. Like Job, I felt I was doing the best I could, yet people kept telling me how broken I was. This led to both confusion and frustration. I knew there were wounds inside, but I kept trying to handle things alone. To make matters worse, when I tried to talk with people about my issues, nobody listened.

In the midst of this turmoil, I began to wonder why I had ever been born—and why I was actually alive. If I had never existed from the beginning, then I wouldn't have had to deal with so many problems.

I finally reached my end and decided I was finished with church and Christian culture. I was done hiding my anger at God.

After voicing my misery, Father God stepped in and began some conversations with me. At first, I was not happy. I wanted Him to give me answers and explain why my childhood had been so difficult. I needed to understand why my experience had been so different from others. What I needed was an explanation, but He wanted to give me affection and love, which actually made my anger worsen.

Father God and I held some heated conversations back and forth. I wanted Him to listen to my cries and change my circumstances. I needed Him to do what *I* wanted.

I remember one time when we were "talking" that I got so angry I started yelling at Him about my past, my hurts, and life. I actually began kicking His shins and blaming Him for all the issues that had occurred in my life.

After I finished, God looked at me, took my face in His hands, and kissed me all over. I raged all the more! In all our debates, He never fixed or changed anything; He just continued to love me.

In all this, He never got mad or punished me. To be honest, I actually expected some sort of rebuke. I had been told my entire life that it was sinful to be mad at God, and I could never come to Him unless I was happy and ready to do everything He wanted. I desired and even expected punishment; instead, He gave me affection.

God continued to treat me with kindness; I eventually grew to see that what I needed was not answers to my problems, but someone to love me and be there for me no matter what. In all my times of yelling and complaints, God remained faithful and listened. I didn't realize it at first, but this eventually began to "fill my empty bucket."

I realized that finding answers did not have to be the driving force behind my happiness. I could allow Him to show me love and give myself permission to be honest with Him because I knew He would not get angry at how I expressed my feelings.

I started going to God to tell Him how I felt and what I thought, even when my feelings and thoughts were uncomfortable. When I waited for punishment to come, it never did.

God did not change the people or situations around me, but He did slowly take care of me. Now when I am bothered by people or situations, I go to Him. I avoid asking questions about my circumstances and instead ask how He plans to take care of me.

Answers do not always come the way I want or in the preferred timing, but I have learned He will take care of me, which is actually what I always needed.

NOTE

1. Graham, Billy. "Where Is Your Hope?" *Daily Devotion* (blog), Billy Graham Evangelistic Association, January 13, 2016, https://billygraham.org/devotion/where-is-your-hope/.

Round Two

MISERABLE COMFORT

*I've had all I can take of your talk. What a
bunch of miserable comforters! Is there no end
to your windbag speeches?*
—JOB 16:2-3

Job and his friends finished speaking. The inside of
the tent was dark. The fire flickered for a moment,
then died to a faint glow. All Trey could hear was the
hustle of distant servants and buzzing flies.

Trey wondered why his master and the others were
so upset. Couldn't they see Job was suffering? What
was so important to them that they needed him
to understand?

Trey decided to head back to his camp and search for food. It had been several hours since his last meal.

Trey lowered the tent corner and crawled back. When he was exiting the tent, a strong hand gripped his shoulder.

"There you are!" The man said. "I have been looking everywhere for you."

Trey looked up at the man's face. It was Uriah, one of his master's head servants.

"Get back to your chores!" He said. "And don't let me catch you napping!"

He shoved Trey and watched him scurry toward camp. Looking back, Trey watched Job's tent disappear from sight. He wondered what Job and his friends were talking about.

Later that night, the servant boys gossiped. Everyone wondered what was going on.

Their master still hadn't returned from Job's tent or taken any food. His attendants started to worry.

Trey settled in as the fires swelled. He and his fellow servants lolling to sleep. The cracks of the fire calmed him. Just as he drifted off, he was awakened by a scream.

AN ATTACK ON ALL SIDES

A client, Ted, sat across from my desk.

"Everything okay?" I asked.

"It's my family. They keep telling me I have problems, but I don't want to hear it."

"What problems are they bringing up?"

"That I'm not living the Christian life. But they can't see how much progress I'm making. I just don't get it." He said, looking down.

This was the first time Ted and I had met. I noticed his lack of eye contact and muffled voice, typical signs for someone dealing with shame and stress.

Ted's wife had called me to schedule an appointment weeks earlier. Warning me over the phone, she said, "Be careful. Ted's a habitual liar. He'll try anything to get out of an uncomfortable situation."

Sitting down with Ted for several minutes, I noticed the deep-seated resentment he felt toward his wife and friends. According to him, they all echoed the same unkind opinion—that he was selfish and rude. Bringing all this to the surface, Ted went on the attack.

"I go to church every Sunday." He said. "I apply the rules and principles but... nothing works. My pastors, my friends, my wife... don't get me."

I sat back and listened; waiting to hear his response. Then I said, "Do you want to ask Father God and see what He thinks about your situation?"

"Father who?"

"Father God. If you're not comfortable with Him, we can ask Jesus or the Holy Spirit."

"I can do Jesus. But I don't know who this Father God is."

"That's fine. We can talk to Jesus if you'd like."

"That'd be nice."

Ted relaxed.

JOB'S FRUSTRATION

In chapter fifteen, Job's friends mount an aggressive attack. Eliphaz goes first and accuses Job of spouting nonsense. No matter what Job says, Eliphaz—like the others—is convinced Job is the problem, and that some hidden sin in his life has brought on such calamity:

> *Would you talk nonsense in the middle of a serious argument,*
> *babbling baloney?*
> *Look at you! You trivialize religion,*
> *turn spiritual conversation into empty gossip.*
> *It's your sin that taught you to talk this way.*
> *You chose an education in fraud*
> (Job 15:3-5).

Eliphaz concludes that Job's sin is motivating the way he speaks, so in addition to feeling ostracized, Job now has to deal with people using his words against him. Like Ted, Job feels attacked on all sides. Not only is Job having to deal with his problems, but he has to challenge his close relationships who are convinced his mind is without reason:

> *Do you think you're the first person to have to*
> *deal with these things?*
> *Have you been around as long as the hills?*
> *Were you listening in when God planned all*
> *this?*
> *Do you think you're the only one who knows*
> *anything?*
> (Job 15:7-8).

Eliphaz accuses Job of allowing his emotions to get the best of him. He asks, Job, is not God enough for you? Don't let your emotions control your temper. Don't you know that everyone sins?

If Eliphaz can get Job to agree with this much (that everyone sins), then he's halfway there. In his mind, Job is being stubborn. If he can admit he's a sinner or at least that some hidden sin has affected his life, then maybe Job can be saved:

> *Are God's promises not enough for you,*
> *spoken so gently and tenderly?*
> *Why do you let your emotions take over,*

lashing out and spitting fire...
(Job 15:11-12).

This is a similar rebuke to what Ted encounters. No matter how well he defends himself, his friends and family point out his frustration and inability to conform to their expectations.

ELIPHAZ'S CREDENTIALS

Eliphaz boosts his rant by showing off his credentials. He points out the wisdom of great men and women that has been handed down to him over the years, which (in his mind) makes him a reliable source:

I've a thing or two to tell you, so listen up!
I'm letting you in on my views;
It's what wise men and women have always taught
holding nothing back from what they were taught
by their parents, back in the days
when they had this land all to themselves...
(Job 15:17-19).

Eliphaz goes on to sermonize on how those who live selfishly receive punishment. People cannot do what they want; they must follow the Lord's commands. Following your own path leads to disobedience, and disobedience (as Job's three friends have seen) leads to judgment:

> *Those who live by their own rules, not God's,*
> *can expect nothing but trouble,*
> *and the longer they live, the worse it gets*
> (Job 15:20).

Much of Eliphaz's statement seems true, but Job doesn't need a sermon on sin or righteousness. He needs to find an answer for his pain.

Job's response points to his friends' inability to bring comfort. "In times like this," Job asserts, "friendship is supposed to bring peace into the situation":

> *I've had all I can take of your talk.*
> *What a bunch of miserable comforters!*
> *Is there no end to your windbag speeches?*
> *What's your problem that you go on and on like*
> *this?*
> *If you were in my shoes,*
> *I could talk just like you.*
> *I could put together a terrific harangue*
> *and really let you have it.*
> *But I'd never do that. I'd console and comfort,*
> *make things better, not worse!*
> (Job 16:2-5).

Job does not fold or let his friends walk over him. He challenges them by saying that if they were in his shoes, their opinions would sound much different.

Job stands against his friends and says, "I don't believe what any of you are saying. Prove to me what you are saying; don't just spout out words of nonsense."

In Job's heart, he knows he is an innocent person; nothing is going to make him back down until God appears and gives him a straight answer. In the midst of attack, Job holds fast to his integrity—even when his circumstances and closest relationships tell him otherwise.

JOB'S COMPLAINT

Job's response to Eliphaz shows that he doesn't like what he is hearing. While Eliphaz may be hearing what Job has to say, the latter's hostility tells us the message received is far from what Job needed.

Throughout Job's story, we see his friends being unable to offer any helpful advice. Rather than hearing Job's cries of *I'm innocent!* each member tries showing why Job is wrong so they can humble him into accepting their opinion.

Doesn't this sound too familiar to any moments you've had in your life? Looking back on Job's situation, I have to wonder. What is God doing this whole time?

While Job and his friend squabble, we don't hear a single word from the Lord. Some may see this as an unwillingness to meddle in humanity's problems, but I wonder if that during this whole section (from the start of Job's troubles to God's appearance) God is listening:

> *And God just stands there and lets them do it,*
> *lets wicked people do what they want with me.*
> *I was contentedly minding my business when*
> *God beat me up.*
> *He grabbed me by the neck and threw me*
> *around*
> (Job 16:11-12).

Job declares that God has to be involved in what is happening. Since He is in control, it is impossible for bad things to happen without His knowledge or participation. If this is the case, how can God be so hard? Job felt, or at least thought he did, like an honest servant of the Lord. Now everything he knows about himself and God is being challenged:

> *Now my face is blotched red from weeping;*
> *look at the dark shadows under my eyes...*
> (Job 16:16).

> *God, you've made me the talk of the town—*
> *people spit in my face;*

I can hardly see from crying so much;
I'm nothing but skin and bones
(Job 17:6-7).

The more Job reflects on his troubles, the more he partners with self-pity. This tends to happen when we focus on the relationships and possessions we lose rather than what the Lord might be doing.

Unfortunately for Job, his friends continue to make the situation worse by offering poor advice:

Maybe you'd all like to start over,
to try it again, the bunch of you.
So far I haven't come across one scrap
of wisdom in anything you've said.
My life's about over. All my plans are smashed,
all my hopes are snuffed out...
(Job 17:10-11).

Up to this point, Job is doing what most of us would do in this situation—complaining! Like Ted, his view of the situation is getting dimmer. Instead of staying silent and waiting on God, he continues to whine.

BILDAD'S RESPONSE

Job's words trigger an interesting response from Bildad, who begins an accusatory tirade and berates Job for rejecting wisdom:

> *How monotonous these word games are getting!*
> *Get serious...*
> *Why do you treat your friends like slow-witted*
> *animals?*
> *You look down on us as if we don't know*
> *anything*
> (Job 18:2-3).

In Bildad's eyes, Job is being selfish. There's all this wisdom around him trying to help, yet he continually rejects all of it! According to Bildad, Job wants the world to revolve around *his* problems. He claims that Job wants the rules changed so the world can exist the way *he* wants it:

> *Why are you working yourself up like this?*
> *Do you want the world redesigned to suit you?*
> *Should reality be suspended to accommodate*
> *you?*
> (Job 18:4).

Similarly, Ted's family confronts him for making everything about *his* problems. They see Ted's disagreements as hard-heartedness and pride. Ted's family echoes Bildad's statement—*how dare you disagree with us on how you should live your life?!* Ted wants to improve but doesn't feel anyone's answers are helping. All he feels is hopelessness and discouragement.

JOB'S REPLY TO BILDAD

In all this, Job refuses to fold. He disregards the accusations and stands true to his integrity. He even goes so far to confront his friends for using his situation to feel superior:

> *How long are you going to keep battering away at me,*
> *pounding me with these harangues?*
> *Time after time after time you jump all over me.*
> *Do you have no conscience, abusing me like this?*
> *Why do you insist on putting me down,*
> *using my troubles as a stick to beat me?*
> *Tell it to God—he's the one behind all this,*
> *he's the one who dragged me into this mess*
> (Job 19:2-3,5-6).

Job tells his friends to talk with God, for He is the one who caused this mess:

He's angry with me—oh, how he's angry!
He treats me like his worst enemy.
He has launched a major campaign against
me...
coming at me from all sides at once
(Job 19:11-12).

Job pleads with his friends to take pity on him and try to understand what is happening. He also decides to give a warning that if it these troubles could happen to him, it could happen to anyone:

Oh, friends, dear friends, take pity on me.
God has come down hard on me!
Do you have to be hard on me too?
Don't you ever tire of abusing me?
(Job 19:21-22).

If you're thinking, "How can we get through to
him,
get him to see that his trouble is all his own
fault?"
Forget it. Start worrying about yourselves.
Worry about your sins and God's coming
judgment,
for judgment is most certainly on the way
(Job 19:28-29).

ZOPHAR'S COMMENT

The next friend to speak is Zophar, and for whatever reason, he is extremely offended. He doesn't understand how Job can be so calloused and goes on a rant to try and educate his friend:

> *I can't believe what I'm hearing!*
> *You've put my teeth on edge, my stomach in a knot.*
> *How dare you insult my intelligence like this!*
> *Well, here's a piece of my mind!*
> *Don't you even know the basics,*
> *how things have been since the earliest days,*
> *when Adam and Eve were first placed on earth?*
> *The good times of the wicked are short-lived;*
> *godless joy is only momentary*
> (Job 20:2-5).

Zophar treats Job like a sinner who has no grid for consequence. He goes back to the age-old reasoning—that evil does exist, but is at best temporary:

> *God will strip them of their sin-soaked clothes*
> *and hang their dirty laundry out for all to see.*
> *Life is a complete wipeout for them,*
> *nothing surviving God's wrath.*
> *There! That's God's blueprint for the wicked—*

what they have to look forward to
(Job 20:27-29).

JOB'S REPLY

Job's reply to Zophar shows his frustration:

Now listen to me carefully, please listen,
at least do me the favor of listening.
Put up with me while I have my say—
then you can mock me later to your heart's
content
(Job 21:2-3).

Job's words show his frustration, but his real problem is not with Eliphaz, Bildad, or Zophar, but with God. Job is angered at the Lord's silence. For all the questions he presents, not a single answer arrives:

It's not you I'm complaining to—it's God.
Is it any wonder I'm getting fed up with his
silence?
(Job 21:4).

Job questions Zophar's statement, and questions why the wicked prosper. When Job looks around, all he sees are the wicked prospering. In his mind, the righteous suffer and the wicked escape punishment:

You might say, "God is saving up the punishment for their children."
I say, "Give it to them right now so they'll know what they've done!"
They deserve to experience the effects of their evil,
feel the full force of God's wrath firsthand
(Job 21:19-20).

Job wants the wicked to suffer so it can appeal to his understanding of how justice works. The biting question of "why does God wait to deal with what is happening?" gets elevated to the forefront:

Naively you claim that the castles of tyrants fall to pieces,
that the achievements of the wicked collapse.
Have you ever asked world travelers how they see it?
Have you not listened to their stories
Of evil men and women who got off scot-free,
who never had to pay for their wickedness?
Did anyone ever confront them with their crimes?
Did they ever have to face the music?
Not likely—they're given fancy funerals with all the trimmings,

Gently lowered into expensive graves,
with everyone telling lies about how wonderful
they were.
So how do you expect me to get any comfort from
your nonsense?
Your so-called comfort is a tissue of lies
(Job 21:28-34).

Again, Job's friends fail to bring wisdom to the situation. Throughout their whole exchange, each has again proven himself to be less than helpful.

TED'S STORY

Back in my office, I asked Ted if he would be willing to feel or sense where Father God was. Ted was at first reluctant because he was afraid this would be just like all the other times when Father God did not show up. I talked about it being a risk and asked if he would be willing to try it out this one last time. Eventually, he agreed.

I asked Ted that if he could not see Father God, would he at least be able to get an impression of where He was. Ted indicated he thought Father God was far away in heaven looking down on him, which I could tell made Ted feel very uncomfortable.

I asked Ted to give himself permission to just sense whatever information Father God presented; he didn't have to believe or accept it just yet.

This appeared to relax Ted, and I asked him how he felt.

"Better," he said. "But I'm still not sure what Father God is going to do."

"Do you have a question you wish to ask Father God? Or would you like me to ask a question for you?"

"You ask." He said and shifted in his seat.

"Okay," I said. "Father God, are you mad or upset with Ted?"

At first, Ted just sat there in silence.

"What did Father God say?"

"What He said can't be right," Ted said. "I'm just hearing wrong."

"Tell me what He said anyway. You might be surprised."

"He said He's not mad or disappointed. That He actually likes me."

"Okay. Why, Father God, why would you even like Ted, if he believes he has been doing all these things wrong as his family and friends have indicated? Father God, are you upset with all the things Ted's indicated?"

Ted sat there for a moment, then shook his head, "He said that I work too hard at trying to do all the right things and that I need to come to Him for help. I keep trying to do everything myself when He wants to help."

"Why, Father God," I asked. "Do you even want to help Ted?"

"Because," Ted said. "I'm His child, and He loves me and wants to be there for me."

After saying this, Ted looked at me and asked with surprise, "Could this be true?"

"Ask Father God," I said.

He did.

"What did He say?"

"Father God said 'Let's go find out by living life.'"

I looked at Ted and asked, "What do you want to do with this information?"

"I'd like to try living life with Father God for once."

Ted left my office planning to discuss with Father God what life could look like. Though he was hesitant at first, pushing through and seeking the Lord led to an incredible breakthrough.

MY STORY

When I used to struggle with issues, the automatic response was to find someone—a leader, family member, or friend—and ask them for insight. Like Job and Ted, these exchanges rarely helped.

I tried sharing my heart and the issues that bothered me, but no one seemed to understand my situation. I explored cell and home groups and even looked for spiritual mothers and fathers. Nothing worked.

Instead of listening to me, people would point out everything wrong in my life. These conversations usually turned to how I was affecting others negatively. Undoubtedly, these talks left me discouraged and without hope.

After years of this, I began to feel desperate. I needed to find someone who could give me understanding, not lectures. I thought I was on a fairly healthy path, but everyone around me said otherwise.

I began to wonder where God was in all this. He had to know what I was going through but every time I tried to seize breakthrough, He failed to step in and fix everything. I was lost and felt completely abandoned.

After I started having honest interactions with Father God, I told Him about my needs of feeling understood and heard. He then showed me how the Holy Spirit could listen to me and teach what I needed to know. So in those situations where I needed help, I asked the Holy Spirit for His wisdom. Soon He was showing what words to say, what strategies to implement into my life, and how to deal with people when they did or said certain things.

For instance, I could be in an uncomfortable situation and not know how to communicate my feelings. I'd simply turn to the Holy Spirit and ask Him what to do, and He would offer suggestions. These suggestions usually told me how to word something I needed, or what to do when I didn't feel safe with others. In each of these times, I felt the Holy Spirit hold my hand while walking through the thick of it.

It was a fascinating process. As I applied His instructions, I watched myself deal with people and situations from a healed place.

Round Three

It's Not Fair!

Job 22–31

*But if Judgment Day isn't hidden from the
Almighty, why are we kept in the dark?
There are people out there getting by with
murder—stealing and lying and cheating.*
—Job 24:1-2

Trey looked around at the men in Job's tent. Their
conversation had been frantic with each member
getting angrier than the last. His master, Eliphaz,
seemed especially upset, but every time he started to
speak, Job raised a hand for silence.

Trey laid down on the ground. His stomach growled.
It had been several hours since his last meal, and the
loud screams that awoke him still rang in his ears.

"How long have I been in here?" Trey thought. "And how long can I stay awake?"

Looking out through a hole in the tent's wall, Trey wondered if he should return to his tent and sleep. The moon was high, and when the sun rose tomorrow, Uriah would call for him and the others to collect wood, draw water, and prepare loaves. The fruitcakes would be out warming in the sun, and if Trey was fast enough, he could sneak in a few bites before dinner.

Trey licked his lips and turned back to Job and his friends. Though their conversations were fierce, Trey always felt safe listening in on their arguments. This was probably because, for once, Trey was not the person being yelled at. In this place, he was merely an invisible listener.

Eliphaz motioned for his friends to remain quiet and moved to the center of the group. His master seemed more agitated now than ever before. By the look on his face, Trey could tell Job and the others were about to receive a very serious talk.

Trey held his stomach and thought of the food he and his friends would prepare tomorrow. How the bread would crack in their hands and the grapes pop in their mouths as they chewed. He dreamt of the meat that would glisten over the fire and the milk that would pool in large wooden bowls.

Trey thought about all this and sighed. Just as he drifted off, Eliphaz started to speak.

JUDGE, JURY, AND EXECUTIONER

It was almost like the TV show, *Intervention*. My client came in trailing an entourage of family members. Each informed me of my client's issues and claimed Sharon, my client, was incapable of telling the truth.

Most of our conversation centered around who should talk first. During the exchange, Sharon just sat there in silence watching her family explain the issues.

First, they said Sharon was an alcoholic. Second, they claimed she would wander through the house while drunk pilfering items when no one was looking.

When Sharon's family confronted her over these issues, they gave her several options—she could either get help and stay at the house, refuse help and move out immediately, or remain home with an observer at all times.

Her father suggested counseling as an option. Somehow, they heard about my work and a month later scheduled a session in my office. I asked if Sharon would feel more comfortable if she and I spoke alone. Her family looked at me as if I had just spoken Chinese and demanded they remain so they could interpret Sharon's logic.

Apparently, no one believed Sharon could be honest about her issues. I asked Sharon again what she wanted. She just looked at me non-caringly and shrugged *whatever*.

Eventually, the family agreed and left the room. After they exited, Sharon and I began our conversation.

At first, Sharon did not want to talk, but I could tell she was hurt. The main problem was she felt her issues were not that big of a deal. She agreed to some of her family's claims but mostly felt her struggles were not that bad. In her mind, lots of people did much, much worse.

According to Sharon, her family too had issues: gossip, lies, superiority. Each of these sins went unpunished, yet here they were pointing out all her "sins."

To make things worse, Sharon had a hard time sensing where God was in all this. She didn't think He was interested in either side of the issue. He certainly was not around to talk with either her or them.

Sharon had the underlying sense that this whole situation was unfair. If God was just, why was she struggling?

JOB'S FRUSTRATION

In chapter twenty-two through thirty-one, Job finds himself in a similar situation. His friends gang up on him by pointing to his "sins" and disregard any defense he brings to the table. Job assures them of his innocence and claims there are far worse people in the world, but his companions fail to see his point and rebuke him for even questioning their advice.

Job wants to know the reason for his punishment, and Eliphaz is happy to provide the answer. Eliphaz states the reason Job is being targeted is because he *deserves it*. He claims God is punishing Job because his sins have reached a boiling point. Job's problem is not that sin exists, but that he is a moral failure in the first place reaping the consequences of his actions:

> *Hardly! It's because you're a first-class moral failure,*
> *because there's no end to your sins.*
> *When people came to you for help,*
> *you took the shirts off their backs, exploited their helplessness...*
> *You turned poor widows away from your door;*
> *heartless, you crushed orphans.*
> *Now you're the one trapped in terror, paralyzed by fear.*
> *Suddenly the tables have turned!*
> (Job 22:5-6; 9-10).

Eliphaz claims that although Job was once on top, his sins have now brought him low. Job's circumstances are then a direct result of his actions.

Job, of course, disagrees with this but not before Eliphaz continues. He lumps Job in with every sinner who rebels against God and questions His authority. In essence, Eliphaz is really trying to paint a picture on the monstrosity of his sin:

> *You agree, don't you, that God is in charge?*
> *He runs the universe—just look at the stars!*
> *Yet you dare raise questions: 'What does God*
> *know?*
> *Are you going to persist in that tired old line*
> *that wicked men and women have always used...*
> *They told God, "Get lost!*
> *What good is God Almighty to us?"*
> *And yet it was God who gave them everything*
> *they had.*
> *It's beyond me how they can carry on like this!*
> (Job 22: 12-13,15,17-18).

I can image Job just sitting there, like Sharon, listening to the accusations. He wants to respond but doesn't have time to—quite yet. Eliphaz is still in the heat of his argument, and if he can convince Job to agree with his perspective, everything will be fine:

> *Give in to God, come to terms with him*
> *and everything will turn out just fine.*
> *Let him tell you what to do;*

take his words to heart.
Come back to God Almighty
and he'll rebuild your life
(Job 22:21-23).

JOB'S SEARCH FOR GOD

Job, ever the stubborn one, refuses to fold to his friend's accusations. He rejects Eliphaz's attempts to categorize him with *true sinners* and stands firm according to his righteousness:

I'm not letting up—I'm standing my ground.
My complaint is legitimate.
God has no right to treat me like this—it isn't
fair!
(Job 23:2).

Job hopes to interact with God personally so he can escape his friends' useless statements. Though his companions have tried, Job knows that only a conversation with God can help. Even in the midst of his pain, Job knows only He can bring answers:

I'd lay my case before him face-to-face,
give him all my arguments firsthand.
I'd find out exactly what he's thinking,
discover what's going on in his head.

Do you think he'd dismiss me or bully me?
No, he'd take me seriously.
He'd see a straight-living man standing before
him;
my Judge would acquit me for good of all charges
(Job 23:4-7).

Job maintains that his righteousness would speak for him. Yet even in the midst of his assuredness, Job feels a flicker of doubt:

I travel East looking for him—I find no one;
then West, but not a trace;
I go North, but he's hidden his tracks;
then South, but not even a glimpse
(Job 23:8-9).

Job reflects on the tragedies that have happened, and fears more may come. He worries that after he gets ahold of God, he may not like the answer:

Is it any wonder that I dread meeting him?
Whenever I think about it, I get scared all over
again.
God makes my heart sink!
God Almighty gives me the shudders!
I'm completely in the dark,
I can't see my hand in front of my face

(Job 23:15-17).

Job begins to unravel how he sees the world. We see his anger at how the righteous suffer while the wicked survive. He wonders if God is even aware of what's going on:

People are dying right and left, groaning in torment.
The wretched cry out for help
and God does nothing, acts like nothing's wrong!
(Job 24:12).

Like Sharon, Job feels a need to point out everyone else's sin. He agrees he is not perfect but says there are so many people out there committing worse sin than him. It doesn't make sense in his mind why *he* is being punished.

HONEST PROCESSING

Bildad responds with a final speech that builds off Eliphaz's lecture. In this sermon, Bildad proclaims that nothing is perfect. Therefore no one—not even Job—should raise questions against God:

God is sovereign, God is fearsome—
everything in the cosmos fits and works in his plan.
Can anyone count his angel armies?
Is there any place where his light doesn't shine?

How can a mere mortal presume to stand up to God?
How can an ordinary person pretend to be guiltless?
Why, even the moon has its flaws,
even the stars aren't perfect in God's eyes,
So how much less, plain men and women—
slugs and maggots by comparison!
(Job 25:2-6).

Bildad argues that Job's pain, although great, is not an issue he should bring before God. Job is human and infinitely small; why should the Lord even listen to his cries?

Job rejects Bildad's aggressive statement and backs his belief that God is the cause for ruin in his life. This might sound blasphemous to his friends, but Job believes (as a man of integrity) that he needs to process his pain honestly and this means getting statements out even at the cost of sounding irreverent. At the core of everything Job does, honesty reigns supreme:

God-Alive! He's denied me justice!
God Almighty! He's ruined my life!
But for as long as I draw breath,
and for as long as God breathes life into me,
I refuse to say one word that isn't true.

I refuse to confess to any charge that's false.
There is no way I'll ever agree to your accusations.
I'll not deny my integrity even if it costs me my life.
I'm holding fast to my integrity and not loosening my grip
and, believe me, I'll never regret it
(Job 27:2-6).

Following this statement, Job presents a challenge to his friends. If they can prove he is wrong, Job is ready to admit it. So far, their ideas have failed miserably. The challenge is on!

Job claims he has given a clear account of his condition and wonders if his friends can see for themselves what God has done, and if so, why they continue to talk in their helpless manner:

I've given you a clear account of God in action,
suppressed nothing regarding God Almighty.
The evidence is right before you. You can all see it for yourselves,
so why do you keep talking nonsense?
(Job 27:11-12).

THE GOOD OLD DAYS

After challenging his friends, Job does what most of us would do—long for "the good old days." Like anyone who has experienced painful seasons, Job desires to return to a time of favor and blessing:

> *Oh, how I long for the good old days,*
> *when God took such very good care of me.*
> *He always held a lamp before me*
> *and I walked through the dark by its light.*
> *Oh, how I miss those golden years*
> *when God's friendship graced my home*
> (Job 29:2-4).

> *When I walked downtown*
> *and sat with my friends in the public square,*
> *Young and old greeted me with respect;*
> *I was honored by everyone in town.*
> *When I spoke, everyone listened;*
> *they hung on my every word.*
> *People who knew me spoke well of me;*
> *my reputation went ahead of me*
> (Job 29:7-10).

Now, Job feels the opposite of everything he hoped for. Blessing has been torn from his grasp:

Now I'm the one they're after,
mistreating me, taunting and mocking.
They abhor me, they abuse me.
How dare those scoundrels—they spit in my
face!
(Job 30:9-10).

I shout for help, God, and get nothing, no
answer!
I stand to face you in protest, and you give me a
blank stare!
You've turned into my tormenter—
you slap me around, knock me about.
You raised me up so I was riding high
and then dropped me, and I crashed.
I know you're determined to kill me,
to put me six feet under
(Job 30:20-23).

Notice, in much of this, that Job addresses God directly. He points out all the troubles he has experienced and dialogues with God much like one would talk with a friend. This, I believe, is the secret to much of Job's success:

What did I do to deserve this?
Did I ever hit anyone who was calling for help?
Haven't I wept for those who live a hard life,

been heartsick over the lot of the poor?
But where did it get me?
I expected good but evil showed up.
I looked for light but darkness fell
(Job 30:24-26).

PRESENTING A CASE

Job takes time to express his case before the Lord. He presents himself as an upstanding and righteous man who does everything for the Lord. Like Sharon, back in my office, he wonders, "Aren't there a whole lot more people doing worse than me? Are my issues really that bad?"

Have I ever left a poor family shivering in the
cold when they had no warm clothes?
(Job 31:19).

Did I set my heart on making big money
or worship at the bank?
(Job 31:24).

I made a solemn pact with myself
never to undress a girl with my eyes
(Job 31:1).

The fear of God has kept me from these things—
how else could I ever face him?

(Job 31:23).

Job tells God, "I've worked hard to follow your rules. Doesn't that mean my life should be filled with blessing?"

> *Isn't calamity reserved for the wicked?*
> *Isn't disaster supposed to strike those who do wrong?*
> (Job 31:3).

Job does not try to run from anything that he has ever done. He never withdraws from his friends because he is afraid of something he has done. In Job's mind, he is the most righteous and respected person on the earth (and according to the Bible, he most likely was). Why, then, was he in so much pain?

> *Oh, if only someone would give me a hearing!*
> *I've signed my name to my defense—*
> *let the Almighty One answer!*
> *I want to see my indictment in writing.*
> *Anyone's welcome to read my defense;*
> *I'll write it on a poster and carry it around town.*
> *I'm prepared to account for every move I've ever made—*
> *to anyone and everyone, prince or pauper*
> (Job 31:35-37).

Job just wants someone to listen to his cries. He is prepared to defend himself but needs someone to bring an adequate answer. Above all else, Job wants to hear from God. Even in his torment, Job knows only one Person can bring true answers.

SHARON'S STORY

Back in my office, I asked Sharon if she would be interested in communicating with Father God. I was interested to see what He would have to say about her "peculiar" situation.

She looked at me, and I could tell she was processing what I was saying.

She said, "Do you think He even cares enough to be around me? Much less talk to me?"

"The only way we can find out," I said. "Is if you go talk to Him personally. But you don't have to do it today if you don't want to. If you want, we can set up another appointment and see how you feel at that time."

I could tell again that she was processing because this was not what she expected to hear. She was expecting me to go after her issues the way her family usually did.

Finally, she said, "Okay. Let's try it."

"Great," I said. "Now close your eyes. Can you see or sense where Father God is?"

She looked at me and was a bit scared. I asked, "What's wrong?"

"Oh, my gosh!" She said. "He's standing right beside me!"

"Is He too close?" I asked, not wanting her to panic. "Would you like me or you to ask Him to take a couple of steps back?"

"No!" She said. "This is amazing! I always thought He didn't care enough to be near me yet here He is."

A little excited, I asked, "What would you like to do now?"

As if on cue, she started to talk and share her feelings, questions, and concerns. Everything flowed out of her like one long speech. I sat there for a couple of minutes, then finally interjected, "Do you mind, telling me what Father God is doing?" I asked.

"Yes," She said, realizing what was actually happening, "Father God is just standing there listening. Sometimes, He's smiling. Other times, He's nodding. This is amazing."

"Why is this amazing?" I said.

"Because," She said, "This is the first time anyone has ever listened to me without trying to correct me."

"May I ask Father God a question?" I said.

She laughed and said, "Father God is saying 'thank you for asking, and yes, you can ask your question.'"

I laughed also and said, "Father God, why would you just stand there?"

She started crying and said, "He says because He loves listening to His daughter."

I asked Father God if He wanted me to be part of the process from that point on; He indicated "No, He would like to spend some time with His daughter."

Sharon left my office not only still talking to God but planning where they could meet on a regular basis.

MY STORY

In my life, people kept approaching me to talk about our relationship. They were friends, usually from church, who felt inspired to tell me everything I was doing wrong. Like Job and Sharon, I felt condemned. All my friends did was tell me how I could be a better Christian, wife, or parent. But it seemed to me that every time I tried to tell my side of the story, no one would listen.

I can agree that some of their points were valid, but looking back, I feel that most of it was religious rhetoric. This even occurred in some of my counseling sessions where I sought therapy.

This led me to becoming mad at God because some of these people were representing Him and they treated me very poorly. Yet whenever I talked to God, He acted very kind and respectfully.

For instance, God never required me to change—He just listened. And sometimes the Holy Spirit would give me insight on how to present my case in times I felt ignored. God didn't need me to change in order to love me. He just sat back and listened.

Then the Holy Spirit would arrive and give me instruction. It was always my choice to decide if I wanted to follow His insight. He began to show me what advice (from people) was correct and which insights I should listen to. But this process started out with me ranting and raving as He listened and comforted me. I couldn't rant and rave to humans because they weren't listening. God ended up being my only option.

Round Four

AGGRESSIVE ADVICE

*If you're so smart, give us a lesson in how to
address God. We're in the dark and can't
figure it out. Do you think I'm dumb enough
to challenge God? Wouldn't that just be
asking for trouble?*
—JOB 37:19-20

Eliphaz and the others fell silent. Trey sank against
the back wall and wondered if they truly had nothing
left to say. It had been a long day filled with heated
conversation. If their anger had finally run out, what
would they talk about now?

Trey felt the cool air rush in from the outside camp. It was still early in the night. If Trey left now, he could make it to his tent and rest well before morning.

Trey lowered himself to the tent's edge and started to crawl out when he heard a man's voice. Trey froze. This person sounded much different than the rest; his voice was louder and more boisterous, like some military commander stepping in to give orders.

Trey turned his gaze to the fire. A man he had never seen before stood beside Job—clothed in bright, untarnished robes. He appeared much younger than the rest.

Trey had not remembered seeing him in the tent. Did he just come in? Or had he, like Trey, been hiding in the shadows the whole time listening?

Like Job, Eliphaz, and the others, this newcomer seemed agitated. He paced back and forth at a frantic speed, his voice not much louder than a hiss.

Trey watched as the man pointed to his listeners, then shook his fist. What was this man so angry about? Who was he? Was he one of Job's friends? If so, why were all of Job's friends so angry? Trey looked at his master, Eliphaz, and waited for him to stop this intruder, but to Trey's surprise, his master said nothing.

Trey marveled at the newcomer's boldness. He had never seen a youth talk to elders in this way. This visitor must have held a lot of authority, but Trey remembered Job was the most influential man in the world;

why would anyone, especially Job, listen to someone like this?

Trey crept back toward the fire—not knowing what to think. So far this trip had been one long mysterious journey. Trey wondered what would happen next. As he approached, the young man's voice grew louder. Now Trey could hear his speech.

HOSTILE COMMUNICATOR

Ray was confused. His new friend, Luke, had become increasingly confrontational. At first, Ray saw their relationship as an opportunity for mentorship, since Luke was nearly fifteen years his junior. But as time went on, it became apparent that Luke enjoyed giving advice much more than receiving it.

Using his "gifts of discernment," Luke began cornering Ray after church to confront him about his sin. Ray was shocked. He had only met Luke three weeks before. What gave him the right or boldness to step forward and make such accusations?

At first, Ray tried to shrug off the conversations, but it only grew worse. Luke was extremely passionate, and every time they spoke, their conversations became more and more heated. Luke was so passionate that it was catching everyone's attention and Ray could only get a few words in per meeting.

The stress from these meetings caused Ray to panic. He found himself shrouded in anxiety—showing up late for work and retreating from his wife and kids.

A few months later, Ray sat in my office. He wanted to process with me and find out how this "innocent" relationship had morphed into something so rotten.

Because of his anxiety, Ray floundered in his connection with God. In addition, he felt insecure about Luke's confidence. Ray had spoken with me years earlier and remembered the breakthrough he encountered. Two weeks later, Ray scheduled a meeting and sat in my office determined to fix whatever issues plagued his life.

ELIHU ARRIVES

In chapter thirty-two, a new character steps onto the scene, Elihu. Out of every character in Job (besides God), he remains the most mysterious. Not much is known about him or the meaning of his visit. Apart from his brief appearance in chapters thirty-two through thirty-seven, Elihu gets no introduction or epilogue. He simply appears, then leaves without explanation.

Elihu's briefness leaves some scholars to theorize that his character is a later addition to the story. Some even believe Elihu is the book's author interjecting his thoughts into the narrative.[1] Both of these insights have yet to be proven, but they remain interesting conjectures.

Whatever the origins of his character, Elihu remains elusive. We do know he is a youth determined to succeed where Job's friends have failed, but even when God confronts Job's friends at the book's conclusion, Elihu is not mentioned. It's as if he disappeared from the story like someone who never existed.

ELIHU'S FIRST SPEECH

Elihu's tactics are aggressive. He is easily the most passionate member of the crew and talks at such a pace that even Job can't seem to interrupt. Like Luke, Elihu feels compelled by God to point out the shortcomings in everyone else. If he, like Luke, can convince his friend of any sins and get him to repent, perhaps he can save him from eternal condemnation.

After his arrival, Elihu goes on the immediate offensive. He attacks Job's friends and their inabilities to reason with Job:

> *I'm a young man,*
> *and you are all old and experienced.*
> *That's why I kept quiet*
> *and held back from joining the discussion*
> (Job 32:6).

In a few short sentences, Elihu gives us some background into his character. He is young, and being so, is likely not permitted to speak before the elders. Following ancient cultural customs, we can assume he stayed silent as long as he could—only raising his voice to speak at the last possible moment.

In an almost frenzy-like state, Elihu begins his presentation:

> *I hung on your words while you spoke,*
> *listened carefully to your arguments.*
> *While you searched for the right words,*
> *I was all ears.*
> *And now what have you proved? Nothing.*
> *Nothing you say has even touched Job*
> (Job 32:11-12).

Elihu presents himself as a man who has answers. Where Eliphaz and the others have failed, Elihu is sure to succeed:

> *Job has yet to contend with me.*
> *And rest assured, I won't be using your arguments!*
> (Job 32:14).

According to Elihu, Job's friends are unable to see what the real issue is, but someone has finally arrived who can answer all. Before continuing, Elihu gives Eliphaz, Bildad, and Zophar one final rebuke:

Do you three have nothing else to say?
Of course you don't! You're total frauds!
(Job 32:15).

Elihu appears to be unable to contain himself. Like Luke, Elihu is someone who is overly aggressive—perhaps a person running on emotions rather than logic. Elihu sees Job's friends as inept and feels he must step in to save the day. As we see, Elihu has a lot of frustrations built up inside, and his following speeches give him an opportunity to release it:

I'm ready to speak my piece...
and it's about time!
I've got a lot to say,
and I'm bursting to say it.
The pressure has built up...
I have to speak—I have no choice...
I'm going to say it straight—
the truth, the whole truth, and nothing but the truth.
I was never any good at bootlicking;
my Maker would make short work of me if I started in now!
(Job 32:17-22).

Elihu's words reveal a man who has tried to remain silent but can no longer contain himself. Elihu silences

Job's friends, then turns his attention to the man himself. Like Luke, Elihu has something to prove. Perhaps he
feels motivated to impress the others with his formida-
ble insight. Whatever his motivation, Elihu is convinced
that God is on his side. He's convinced he will be able to
provide the wisdom that is needed. In this mindset, Elihu
begins his speech:

> *What I'm about to say*
> *has been carefully thought out.*
> *I have no ulterior motives in this;*
> *I'm speaking honestly from my heart.*
> *The Spirit of God made me what I am,*
> *the breath of God Almighty gave me life!*
> (Job 33:2-4).

He then uses empathy to try and break down any
restraints that separate him and Job. Elihu is truly wise in
this regard. If he can get Job to empathize with him, he
will be more willing to listen:

> *And if you think you can prove me wrong, do it...*
> *Look, I'm human—no better than you...*
> *So let's work this through together;*
> *don't let my aggressiveness overwhelm you*
> (Job 33:5-7).

Elihu then moves on to lay out his qualifications. He's determined to make Job know he is a reasonable, safe place to process pain.

After laying out his credentials and doing his best to lower Job's guard, he launches in full force:

> *Here's what you [Job] said.*
> *I heard you say it with my own ears.*
> *You said, "I'm pure—I've done nothing wrong.*
> *Believe me, I'm clean—my conscience is clear..."*
> *But let me tell you, Job, you're wrong...*
> *God is far greater than any human.*
> *So how dare you haul him into court,*
> *and then complain that he won't answer your*
> *charges?*
> *God always answers, one way or another,*
> *even when people don't recognize his presence*
> (Job 33:8-9; 12-14).

Elihu states that because God is sovereign, it's impossible for Job to know the reasons for his tragedy. He claims God is at work even when we don't recognize or accept it. Elihu says the Lord works through dreams and visions, uses pain to catch our attention, and communicates with us directly through prayer (see Job 33:15-26). If Job cannot see God's hand in the midst of this crisis, maybe it is because he is not partnering with trust:

This is the way God works.
Over and over again.
He pulls our souls back from certain destruction
so we'll see the light—and live in the light!
(Job 33:29-30).

Elihu claims Job's sin is a blessing in disguise. If Job will just humble himself and repent, God will bring him back to full restoration.

At this point, Job tries to answer Elihu, but the young man refuses to stop. I can imagine him afraid of losing his train of thought, continuing forward so no one can stop him:

Keep listening, Job.
Don't interrupt—I'm not finished yet.
But if you think of anything I should know, tell
me.
There's nothing I'd like better than to see your
name cleared.
Meanwhile, keep listening. Don't distract me
with interruptions.
I'm going to teach you the basics of wisdom
(Job 33:31-33).

Elihu continues to frame himself as a man filled with wisdom. He assures everyone his insight is in fact directly brought to him from the Lord, but this is exactly what Eliphaz, Bildad, and Zophar kept saying for the last thirty chapters. How will this, then, be any different?

ELIHU'S SECOND SPEECH

Once Elihu begins his second speech, he realizes he cannot convince Job of his sin on his own. So after hurling out insults, Elihu decides to re-enlist the help of the friends:

> *Isn't it just common sense—*
> *as common as the sense of taste—*
> *To put our heads together*
> *and figure out what's going on here?*
> (Job 34:3-4).

Elihu points out that Job is in the wrong. God is incapable of doing evil, so Job *has* to be the reason for his tragedy. Although this information comes out eloquently, it is hard to ignore how similar this sounds to Eliphaz's and Zophar's arguments:

> *We've all heard Job say, "I'm in the right,*
> *but God won't give me a fair trial..."*
> *It's impossible for God to do anything wicked...*
> *He's the one who runs the earth!*
> *He cradles the whole world in his hand!*
> *If he decided to hold his breath,*

every man, woman, and child would die for
lack of air
(Job 34:5; 13-15).

Elihu states God cannot be wicked, so there must only be one conclusion—everything is Job's fault. Deducing this, Elihu asks, "Job, why aren't you listening?"

So, Job, use your head;
this is all pretty obvious...
Do you dare condemn the righteous, mighty
God?
(Job 34:16-17).

Elihu goes on to say that God can do whatever He wants. If He wants to answer our cries, He will. If He chooses to punish us, so be it. God is the one in charge, and we need to agree with His sovereignty no matter what. If we fail to do so, we partner with sin:

If God is silent, what's that to you?
If he turns his face away, what can you do about it?
But whether silent or hidden, he's there, ruling...
So why don't you simply confess to God?
Say, "I sinned, but I'll sin no more.
Teach me to see what I still don't see.
Whatever evil I've done, I'll do it no more"
(Job 34:29-32).

Elihu wants Job to admit his wrongdoing and confess any sin. Even if he doesn't know what sin he has partnered with, asking God will reveal an answer. Like Luke, Elihu wants his "mentor figure" to confess and repent. But Job seems to keep elevating himself to a higher position. If Job is on the same level as all creation, why does he continue to partner with confidence and assuredness? Elihu sees Job's stubbornness as pride and rebukes him for standing with this opinion. He has a few more tricks up his sleeve, and he's going to try them:

> *Just because you refuse to live on God's terms,*
> *do you think he should start living on yours?*
> *Job...you've compounded your original sin by...*
> *piling up indictments against the Almighty One*
> (Job 34:33, 36-37).

Elihu continues his assault on Job's character, but the latter won't listen. I can imagine now, by this time, Elihu is growing quite frustrated.

ELIHU'S FINAL SPEECH

Elihu begins his final speech with an assault on Job's logic. If he can't appeal to him emotionally, he'll try to win rationally:

> *Does this kind of thing make any sense?*
> *First you say, "I'm perfectly innocent before*

God."

And then you say, "It doesn't make a bit of difference whether I've sinned or not"
(Job 35:2-3).

Elihu asks Job to consider how his logic affects God. Whether someone's good or bad, does it really matter in the Almighty's eyes? Since our actions don't affect God, is He really impressed when we are good and disappointed when we are bad?

> *If you sin, what difference could that make to God?*
>
> *No matter how much you sin, will it matter to him?*
>
> *Even if you're good, what would God get out of that?*
>
> *Do you think he's dependent on your accomplishments?*
>
> *The only ones who care whether you're good or bad are your family and friends and neighbors.*
>
> *God's not dependent on your behavior*
> (Job 35:6-8).

Elihu points out how people treat God. They call to Him when there is trouble; otherwise, they ignore Him. With this in mind, why should God notice Job in his torment? If He disregards the cries of sinners who ignore

Him when things go well, then why should He hear Job?
What makes him so special?

> *When times get bad, people cry out for help.*
> *They cry for relief from...*
> *But never give God a thought when things go*
> *well...*
> *People are arrogantly indifferent to God—*
> *until, of course, they're in trouble...*
> *There's nothing behind such prayers except*
> *panic;*
> *the Almighty pays them no mind.*
> *So why would he notice you*
> *just because you say you're tired of waiting to be*
> *heard...*
> (Job 35:9-10; 12-15).

The Message Bible says Elihu *"took a deep breath, but
kept going..."* (Job 36:1). I imagine this man is frantic,
doing his best to keep the conversation going. I envision
him almost afraid—like if anyone stops him, he'll lose his
thoughts. All this information flows quickly, with Elihu
maybe not even knowing what exactly is coming from
his mouth:

> *Stay with me a little longer. I'll convince you.*
> *There's still more to be said on God's side.*
> *I learned all this firsthand from the Source...*

(Job 36:2-3).

Elihu believes God is the source of all his wisdom and challenges Job or anyone else to stand against it. He states the Lord is for the good but against the wicked. Therefore, if God is against you, then there must be sin in your life provoking an attack:

> *It's true that God is all-powerful,*
> *but he doesn't bully innocent people.*
> *For the wicked, though, it's a different story—*
> *he doesn't give them the time of day,*
> *but champions the rights of their victims.*
> *He never takes his eyes off the righteous;*
> *he honors them lavishly, promotes them*
> *endlessly*
> (Job 36:5-7).

Elihu's mind works with a simple formula: God is good, and the wicked are bad; therefore, God cannot be bad so everything bad must be due to some wickedness.

According to Elihu, Job needs to receive all this advice that has been offered. If he will just submit and accept his situation, God will bring salvation:

> *But those who learn from their suffering,*
> *God delivers from their suffering.*
> *Oh, Job, don't you see how God's wooing you*

from the jaws of danger?
How he's drawing you into wide-open places—
inviting you to feast at a table laden with
blessings?
Above all, don't make things worse with more
evil—
that's what's behind your suffering as it is!
(Job 36:15-16,21).

Elihu then launches into the awesomeness of God, His workmanship, and what He created. In all this, Elihu asks, "Do you understand what you are saying or to Whom you are saying it to?" If Job did, would he even bring his complaints before the Almighty?

If you're so smart, give us a lesson in how to
address God.
We're in the dark and can't figure it out.
Do you think I'm dumb enough to challenge
God?
Wouldn't that just be asking for trouble?
(Job 37:19-20).

Elihu then concludes that Job's next action should be to praise and acknowledge God's goodness:

Mighty God! Far beyond our reach!
Unsurpassable in power and justice!

It's unthinkable that he'd treat anyone unfairly.
So bow to him in deep reverence, one and all!
If you're wise, you'll most certainly worship him
(Job 37:23-24).

Job never answers or is not allowed to answer Elihu. Once the young man finishes his speech, God intervenes.

RAY'S STORY

Back in my office, I asked Ray what he thought his issue was, or if it was a total mystery.

He said he had no idea and he was not hearing anything from Father God. This scared him even more.

"Do you have any idea where Father God is right now?" I asked. "Is He up in heaven, in the hallway, or maybe here in the office?"

Ray shook his head, "I have no idea."

"Do me a favor," I said. "And just sense where He could be, even if it seems faint."

Ray closed his eyes and said, "He could possibly be in the office lobby."

"Alright," I said. "What do you sense is the expression on His face?"

Ray sat in silence for a moment, then said, "He is looking at me, wondering what I need or want."

"Ask Him," I said. "What do you need or want?"

Ray thought for a moment, then said, "I want to know what I did wrong to make this relationship turn out so bad? Am I really as bad a person as Luke says? Is God mad at me because I couldn't love or be the godly person Luke expected me to be?"

"Would you like to ask God those questions? Or would you like me to?"

"I can do it," Ray said, but I could tell he was not sure if he wanted to hear the answers.

"What if you just ask Father God and see what He has to say? You can decide later what you want to do about the information."

"Okay," Ray said. "God, am I really as bad of a person as Luke says?"

I watched as Ray listened to Father God—shock spreading over his face.

"What did Father God say?"

Ray sat still with the same shocked expression, "He asked me why I didn't come to Him after Luke said those things? I looked at God and said 'I never thought about asking You. I thought You'd agree with Luke.'"

"How does that make you feel?"

"I'm not sure," Ray said. "I feel confused."

"Why do you feel confused? Maybe you should let Father God know how you feel about His answer."

Ray and Father God then had a conversation about how he felt confused. He asked God about what to do when people said he was not being the godly leader they expected.

God told Ray he was doing a good job but ventured the idea that maybe he think about the needs Luke and others wanted and were looking for, and why they were going to Ray to meet them. The Lord suggested that Ray bring people to Him ultimately to get their needs met.

Ray liked this arrangement. He left my office knowing his connection with Father God was still there and knowing He was going to be with him to help others have a connection with the Lord.

MY STORY

Like Ray, we all have people—family, friends, and acquaintances—who share their thoughts and feelings about us. They want us to know about our issues and sins so we can correct them and better hear what the Lord says.

Like Elihu, these people love to let us know about their knowledge of God. They feel compelled to inspire others to live a life in a manner the Bible indicates.

Years ago, a team and I were conducting training in a small church. At the beginning of my first day of training, a lady came up and said the Lord told her I had a spirit of rebellion like witchcraft and that I had to take care of it.

At first, I was shocked. I looked at Father God and asked Him what to do. He just smiled and said not to worry about it. I calmed down.

I thanked the lady for letting me know her information. I then said I could certainly see how she saw rebellion in me. We had a conversation the day before and thinking back on it; I realized I must have said something about inner healing that she felt was not correct theology.

The lady asked me, "What do you plan to do about your rebellion?"

"Nothing right now," I said.

She looked at me in disgust.

"At this point," I said "God has not indicated that I need to change anything."

"The Lord told me that you need to do something about it, and it needs to happen now!"

"Well," I said. "Why don't you go back to Father God and ask Him what I need to do about it. Cause right now I'm not feeling anything."

The woman scoffed and walked away. I could tell she wasn't happy.

I turned to Father God and said, "You better protect me because she'll be sitting in the front row frowning and asking hard questions."

By the end of the day, I realized she had smiled the whole time and never asked one single question.

I realized I could have changed for her and for many others as well, but if Father God was not involved with this change, then I would be doing it out of my own strength. If Father God suggested the change and was part of the process, then I would have had the grace and strength to do it.

Later, I talked with a person who had permission to speak into my life. She also indicated that rebellion was a part of my life. I went back to Father God and asked what He thought about this rebellion. He indicated He was aware of it but didn't need me to solve it at this time. What I did need to be aware of was how my actions and attitudes that could be viewed as rebellion affected others around me.

Aspects of who I am should never be in control, but I should be in control of them. There are times when who I am has a negative effect on the situation, but this does not mean I have lost who I am. All it means is I need to take a step back and show respect to the relationships around me.

NOTE

1. Summary and Analysis Job," *CliffsNotes*, https://www. cliffsnotes.com/literature/o/old-testament-of-the-bible/ summary-and-analysis/job.

Round Five

GOD'S RESPONSE

Job 37–42

Where were you when I created the earth?...
Who decided on its size? Certainly you'll know
that! Who came up with the blueprints and
measurements...While the morning stars sang
in chorus and all the angels shouted praise?
—JOB 38:4-5, 7

The tent's doors flew open, ushering in a massive, guttural breeze. The young man, who had just finished speaking, fell back against its weight.

Trey shielded his eyes and braced himself against the floor. The tent's walls shook. The poles cracked and rattled where they stood.

Job, Eliphaz, and the others shielded their faces. Dust swirled around them.

"What's happening?" One of Job's friends asked.

"Judgment!" Eliphaz said. "From God."

Another breeze flew in and tossed them to the ground.

Trey peered through the swirling grime. Job was the only one not afraid. He held his place, kneeling before the gust like some friend awaiting a long-desired visitor.

The gale picked up and centered itself around the fire, creating a column of soot and flame. Now the heat was growing—and it was becoming unbearable.

"Job." A powerful voice said. It echoed through the tent and shook Trey's bones. It was like nothing Trey had ever heard. It was both soft and fearsome, reassuring yet terrifying.

Trey watched as Job drew closer to the fire. He wondered if he should try and save Job before the flames devoured him.

Trey tried to lift himself off the ground, but the heat was too great. He sank back into the soil—the storm's intensity growing. Before Trey closed his eyes, the last thing he saw was Job disappearing inside the cyclone.

DESPERATION

A new client, Mary, called to set up an appointment.

"Everything alright?" I asked.

"No." She said. "I need to schedule an appointment right away. It's an emergency."

We went on to schedule a meeting for the following week. When the time came, she arrived twenty minutes late.

"I'm so sorry," she said, hurrying in. "I just don't know how to talk about my problems."

"What problems are bothering you?"

"It's just...I'm not sure if I need counseling or... information."

Mary went on to say that she was afraid. She didn't know if she needed help from an inner healing counselor or a church pastor.

"We can cancel if you want," I said.

"No," she said. "Let's just try it and see what happens."

Mary opened up and told me about some of her strange encounters with God. He kept saying things that didn't make sense, and Mary wasn't sure what to do with His information. Some days she felt He was celebrating her. Other times He sounded mad.

This inconsistency led Mary to think that maybe God was trying to tell her something important, but another voice was getting in the way. Mary needed help, and she wasn't sure how to tell which voice was God's.

"Well," I said. "What would you like to do with all this information?"

With tears in her eyes, she confessed, "I don't know."

I asked Mary who she thought the conflicting voices were. This question frightened Mary; it made her ask, *If God's not talking to me, then who is?*

We began our session by working through Mary's perception of herself and her relationship with the Lord. The voices she kept hearing made her see life in a slanted manner. This is why she needed to talk with someone. The beliefs she had about God were being challenged. She needed a direct encounter with the Lord so He could sort things out.

ELIHU'S FINAL STATEMENT

Before God speaks, Elihu wraps up his final statement:

> *Mighty God! Far beyond our reach!*
> *Unsurpassable in power and justice!*
> *It's unthinkable that he'd treat anyone unfairly.*
> *So bow to him in deep reverence, one and all!*
> *If you're wise, you'll most certainly worship him*
> (Job 37:23-24).

The Bible does not make it clear if Job ignores Elihu, or if God's sudden appearance simply disrupts the conversation. No one knows if Job has an answer for Elihu or if Job thinks Elihu's opinion isn't worthy of a response.

Whatever the reason, Elihu's arguments don't receive any sort of response. God instead intervened, and Elihu disappears. God begins His side of the story, and everyone listens.

GOD CONFRONTS JOB

The Bible says God answers Job out of a whirlwind. In the original Hebrew, the word *whirlwind* means "tempest, storm, or whirlwind."[1] In the online dictionary, *tempest* is "a violent windstorm, especially one with rain, hail, or snow."[2] *Whirlwind* means "any circling rush or violent onward course."[3] Looking at these definitions, we can assume God's visit is far from peaceful.

God speaks for the next four chapters and doesn't bother to address anyone but Job. He doesn't explain Job's issues or the accusations laid against Him. He only asks Job where he was when the universe was created. He tells Job the origin of all things—from nature to animals and everything else—and reminds him how He, God Almighty, was involved from its beginning:

Why do you confuse the issue?
Why do you talk without knowing what you're
talking about...
I have some questions for you
and I want some straight answers...
Where were you when I created the earth?
Tell me, since you know so much!
Who decided on its size...
Who came up with the blueprints and
measurements...
...while the morning stars sang in chorus
and all the angels shouted praise?
(Job 38:2-7).

God does not address Job's pain or the meaning of his struggles. He instead challenges Job with a simple question, "Who are you, Job, to accuse me of anything?"

Do you know where Light comes from
and where Darkness lives...
Have you ever traveled to where snow is made...
Can you teach the lioness to stalk her prey
and satisfy the appetite of her cubs?
(Job 38:19,22,39).

Are you the one who gave the horse his prowess...
Was it through your know-how that the hawk

learned to fly...
(Job 39:19,26).

God's tone in all this is far from comforting in the expected sense. He doesn't reassure Job by saying, "You're right. You have every good reason to be upset. How can I help?" Instead, God confronts Job for even questioning His ability to judge correctly and rule the universe:

> *Now what do you have to say for yourself?*
> *Are you going to haul me, the Mighty One, into*
> *court and press charges?*
> (Job 40:2).

This is probably not the interaction Job was hoping for, but he nevertheless takes the opportunity to repent and embrace humility:

> *I'm speechless, in awe—words fail me.*
> *I should never have opened my mouth!*
> *I've talked too much, way too much.*
> *I'm ready to shut up and listen*
> (Job 40:4-5).

Whether this epiphany is reached through fear or panic, we do not know. Somehow Job begins to see things differently. He no longer focuses on how *he* views a subject. He instead chooses to focus on his situation according to God's perspective.

MORE QUESTIONS FROM GOD

After Job repents for talking too much and not listening, God continues His questions:

> *Do you presume to tell me what I'm doing wrong?*
> *Are you calling me a sinner so you can be a saint?*
> *Do you have an arm like my arm?*
> *Can you shout in thunder the way I can?*
> *Go ahead....*
> *Let's see...*
> *Unleash your outrage.*
> *Target the arrogant and lay them flat...*
> *Dig a mass grave and dump them in it...*
> *I'll gladly step aside and hand things over to you—*
> *you can surely save yourself with no help from me!*
> (Job 40:8-14).

God's correction shines through in this passage. He challenges Job by saying, "If you can prove that I am wrong, I will gladly step aside and let you take the reins." Since the beginning of this story, Job has been questioning God and saying that He isn't doing a good job. God confronts these statements by inviting Job to have a chance at it:

Look at the land beast, Behemoth, I created
him as well as you...
But you'd never want him for a pet—
you'd never be able to housebreak him
(Job 40:15, 24).
Or can you pull in the sea beast, Leviathan,
with a fly rod and stuff him in your creel?
If you can't hold your own against his glowering
visage,
how, then, do you expect to stand up to me?
Who could confront me and get by with it?
I'm in charge of all this—I run this universe!
(Job 41:1; 10-11).

God concludes His speech by stating His position in the universe. No one else runs it but Him. No one else can subdue the creatures He has created. No one being is powerful enough to challenge His authority.

In all this, God does not explain anything that has happened to Job. He does not step in to defend Himself or explain why any of the tragedies happened. Nor does He answer any of Job's or his friends' questions. Instead, God describes what's in His hands—*everything*.

JOB'S FINAL REPLY

Job's final response shows he has received the message. Hearing God speak, he no longer desires to partner with self-pity or accusation. Job is finished hurling blame. He is instead ready to listen:

> *I'm convinced: You can do anything and everything.*
> *Nothing and no one can upset your plans.*
> *You asked, "Who is this muddying the water,*
> *ignorantly confusing the issue, second-guessing my purposes?"*
> *I admit it. I was the one. I babbled on about things far beyond me,*
> *made small talk about wonders way over my head.*
> *You told me, "Listen, and let me do the talking.*
> *Let me ask the questions. You give the answers."*
> *I admit I once lived by rumors of you;*
> *now I have it all firsthand—*
> *from my own eyes and ears!*
> (Job 42:2-5).

Job confesses that he now has to look at himself and see how he is contributing to his problems. Job takes responsibility for his thoughts and actions. His final comment to God is:

*I'm sorry—forgive me. I'll never do that again,
I promise!
I'll never again live on crusts of hearsay, crumbs
of rumor*
(Job 42:6).

The King James Version states it differently:

*Wherefore I abhor myself and repent in dust
and ashes* (Job 42:6 KJV).

Job now understands his connection with God and
the reality of his world. Job used to live on rumors of God,
but now he has firsthand information. To put it in my
own terminology, Job finally has an intimate and honest
relationship with the Lord. With this new relationship,
Job can work with God to find out answers and truth for
the reality of his life.

CONCLUSION

After Job repents, God turns to Eliphaz, Bildad,
and Zophar:

*I've had it with you and your two friends... You
haven't been honest either with me or about
me—not the way my friend Job has. Take seven
bulls and seven rams, and go to my friend Job.
Sacrifice a burnt offering on your own behalf.*

My friend Job will pray for you and I will accept
his prayer. He will ask me not to treat you as
you deserve for talking nonsense about me, and
for not being honest with me, as he has
(Job 42:7-8).

Out of everyone in the story, Eliphaz, Bildad, and Zophar appear to be the ones offering sound, biblical advice. Yet in this passage, God declares Job—the guy who couldn't stop complaining—as the one being honest? How is this possible?

Even in his darkest moments, Job remains honest about how he feels. He stays steadfast in his pursuit of God.

Job's friends, meanwhile, try to find blame in everyone but themselves. They never self-examine to see if they add to the situation. Obviously, this doesn't impress the Lord.

God instructs the three friends to have Job sacrifice an offering and pray for them so that God will not treat them as they deserve since they were not honest/correct about who God is.

Interestingly, God never mentions Elihu. Nor does He include him in the order to go to Job to be included in the sacrifice God indicated for the other three friends.

Elihu is never mentioned by God or anyone else after his final speech. He instead vanishes.

After Job conducts the sacrifice and prayer for his friends, God restores his fortunes. Job's brothers, sister, and friends come to celebrate with him and bring comfort because of all the troubles he has experienced.

At the end of his journey, Job's life and fortune became more blessed than ever, so much so that he lived another 140 years, *"Then he died—an old man, a full life"* (Job 42:17). A full life with firsthand knowledge of God can be ours.

MARY'S STORY

As I talked with Mary about her need for a direct encounter with God, she said that she felt unworthy to have a direct encounter with God.

I stopped her and said, "That does not feel good, does it?"

She folded her arms and said, "No, it doesn't!"

"Then that thought cannot be from Father God because Father God does not make us feel bad. Even when He shows us issues that need to be dealt with. Father God does not bring guilt or shame, only peace. So if your thoughts bring guilt, shame, or make you feel bad, then it is not God."

After saying this, I could feel Mary relax. I asked her, "Do you want to go interact with Him to see what He wants to let you know instead?"

"Yes." She said.

"Great. Do you have a sense or feeling of where Father God is right now?"

She thought for a moment, then said, "Yes. He is sitting in the chair beside me."

"Okay," I said. "How does this make you feel?"

"On edge. I can't tell if this is really true. I, mean, can I even trust what I am seeing?"

"Good point," I said. "Besides feeling on edge, is there anything else you're sensing?"

"Yes," She said. "But I'm afraid to believe it."

"Don't worry about believing it right now. Just tell me what it is."

"It's like a calmness, not quite peaceful, but calm."

"What are your thoughts about this feeling?"

Slowly, a grin curved across her face, "I like it."

"Then let's focus on that feeling. What would you like to ask Father God?"

Mary thought for a moment, then started asking questions to Father God and I watched her relax. At one point, I said, "I don't mean to interrupt but how is what you are hearing making you feel?"

"Very good," Mary said, her face beaming with a smile.

"Are you getting your questions answered?"

"Yes," She said. "And I understand about the confusing thoughts and voices now. Father God indicated I was so afraid of being wrong that I started listening to my fears instead of Him."

Father God and Mary finished their conversation. She indicated she was excited to know the difference between her thoughts and His.

MY STORY

It was my first training trip to a certain European country, and I had just landed and been taken to an elaborate garden. As I stood on the steps overlooking its beauty, I glanced down at my purse and noticed my wallet was missing.

I looked at Father God and indicated that I did not feel safe. I let my hosts know what happened and we started looking right away. The more we looked, the madder I grew.

"This isn't fair!" I thought. "All my money and credit cards are gone!"

All the stories about identify fraud flooded over me. I became very scared.

As I walked around, I let Father God know exactly how I felt. I told Him that He had promised to protect me, but with my wallet stolen, I definitely did not feel protected. I had no money, no credit cards, and all the fears of having someone steal my identity.

Worst of all, the fear of "See? Here we go again. God told me I would be protected, but it's not true" starting seizing me.

I then stopped and realized I had a choice. I could either continue to melt down in panic or I choose to see what Father God was going to do.

I looked at Him and said, "I'm going to step back and allow You to protect me. I'm still upset about my wallet being stolen, but I will stop focusing on what is happening and start looking for what You are going to do."

In my case, it was to continue to view the garden and then going to lunch. Once I made that choice, the shaking in my body and negative thoughts calmed down.

At lunch, I joked about my wallet being stolen, and how everyone else had to pay for any expenses I accrued during the week. Every once in a while, my thoughts would turn negative, but every time I'd say, "Nope. We are waiting on Father God."

When the training started, our hosts told the congregation that my wallet had been stolen. A lady came up after a session and said, "You must have felt so violated."

I thought about this and said, "No, actually, I didn't."

At that point, Father God tapped me on the shoulder and said, "See? That is how I protected you—emotionally."

I realized that even though I was staying in a hotel room alone all week, I did not feel like someone was going to break in and harm me. I also was not looking around every time I walked around in crowded areas, fearing another theft. I recognized that what I needed was emotional safety, and God provided it.

"Thanks," I said to God. "I will take being protected emotionally."

He then showed me a picture of me at the top of the stairs in the garden. He told me that if I had been aware of someone close enough to take my wallet, I would have turned and alarmed the person, who could have pushed me down the steps to get away. This could have badly injured or even killed me.

Similar to Job in his conversation with God, this was not the outcome I expected or wished for. I wanted my wallet not to be stolen, and not to have to deal with the situation or its fears. I wanted to feel protected by having none of it happen. But that is not how the day went.

I don't know why everything happened the way it did. People said, "Look at the lesson you learned!" I think I could have learned the lessons in a different way. All I know is that when I decided to allow Father God to protect me, He did.

NOTES

1. Lexicon: Strong's H5591 – *ca 'ar*, s.v. "Whirlwind," Blue Letter Bible, accessed January 5, 2018, https://www.blueletterbible.org/lang/lexicon/lexicon.cfm?Strongs=H5591&t=ESV.

2. Dictionary.com, s.v. "Tempest," accessed January 5, 2018, http://www.dictionary.com/browse/tempest?s=t.

3. Dictionary.com, s.v. "Whirlwind," accessed January 5, 2018, http://www.dictionary.com/browse/whirlwind?s=t.

A Full Life

Trey threw the last of his supplies onto the cart. The sun was beaming down on his face. Looking back, he saw his master bow before Job, then climb onto his own cart to join the column.

Trey looked ahead. There was a vast army of people ahead of him and behind. All those who had come to visit Job were finally going home.

Trey snapped his reins, and the oxen pulled forward. As he moved, Trey thought about the storm and Job's conversation with God. He was not sure how to feel or what to think. Everyone around him had different opinions. Some were terrified; others denied its existence altogether.

His master, Eliphaz, was obviously shaken. It did not take long for him to send for the best bulls in camp afterward to appease his friend. When the ceremony ended, Trey watched his master relax and repent. Truly something had changed.

Many people in Eliphaz's camp were unsure of what happened. Some wondered if God's intervention was really going to change anything. Others like Trey decided to wait and watch it all play out once they returned home.

There was a group of people who claimed they heard nothing. They thought all this talk of God was nonsense. They didn't hear, see, or sense anything. All they experienced was a storm that frightened their livestock and destroyed some tents. Several of these people thought Eliphaz's sacrifice was a waste of good livestock, but having to follow orders, they delivered the bulls up anyway.

Trey snapped his reins and looked ahead; he knew something was different. He had heard God's voice and felt something shift inside of him. He was not sure what it was, but he had a long road ahead to figure it out.

Trey had seen a lot during his trip. He had seen new lands, new people, and a man's encounter with God. From this day on, Trey knew his life would never be the same.

I HOPE YOU HAD AN INTERESTING TIME JOURNEYING with me through Job. Before we end, let me point out what God said in the first few chapters:

> *God said to Satan, "Have you noticed my friend Job? There's no one quite like him, is there— honest and true to his word, totally devoted to God and hating evil? He still has a firm grip on his integrity! You tried to trick me into destroying him, but it didn't work"* (Job 2:3).

It is important to know that God was not looking for any reason to punish Job; it was satan who attempted to trick God. Everything bad in this story came from the devil's attempts to *trick* God into severing His connection with Job; but as usual, the devil's plans didn't work.

Whoever wrote this book made poetry out of our whining. Job's wife didn't want to deal with the effects on her life from Job's situation. She instead wanted to end her and her husband's misery by getting rid of God. Job's friends wanted to end their torment by hiding themselves in their own understanding of who God was. In all the book's dialogues, Job refused to curse God; he remained honest and faithful and pursued truth even during the highest points of his misery. He never received any answers on why he was suffering nor did he learn how he could avoid it in the future.

This lack of an answer on human tragedy can be frustrating for some audiences. People want tragedies explained so they can avoid them in the future. If there is a formula, we want it; but we should be careful not to think like Job's friends who presumed "they" could fix the issue. In the case of Job, the reason for human suffering is and remains a mystery; a mystery even God refuses to give a clear-cut answer.

There is more to the book of Job than just people trying to understand pain. If we examine his reactions, we see him first rage in pain and protest but become silent and awestruck when God appears.

So, what is the solution to this mystery? Why do good people suffer? Did Job have to go through all his pain to receive a deeper connection with God?

Perhaps we should examine his suffering, "participating insofar as we are able" so we can "[endure] the mystery [as we search] for God" (The Message Bible, intro to Job by Eugene H. Peterson). The inner healing ministry that I lead deals with wounds and lies that prevent people from connecting with God, but it does not stop suffering from happening in the first place.

We will continue to experience difficult events, situations, and feelings in the future. My question is: "What are you going to do about it?" What I want is for people to go and have that connection with God to see what He reveals.

So, what are we going to do about this mystery in the book of Job? Perhaps it will inspire us to analyze our own relationships with the Lord. Or maybe it will lure us into a conversation that challenges preconceived notions about God's sovereignty. I want you to think about how you relate to Job's story. Do you see it as a discussion on human suffering? Or an exploration of one man's journey toward inner healing—a journey that can lead to an honest relationship with God through firsthand knowledge of Him?

Maybe it's time we all looked at Job differently. We can use it as inspiration to deal with our wounds and lies, and the useless advice people tell us when they "think" they're helping. If we look at Job's story as an inner healing manual, maybe we can work through our obstacles and focus on what really matters—God's perspective. Maybe then we can receive what Job discovered—a full life.

Final Round

My friend Job will pray for you, and I will
accept his prayer. He will ask me not to treat you
as you deserve for talking nonsense about me,
and for not being honest with me, as he has.
—Job 42:8

We have come to the end of Job's and Trey's stories—and the tales of each client in my office—but we have yet to finish *my story*. I still have conversations with Father God, Jesus, and Holy Spirit because I have needs that need to be met—and I still have to deal with life and reality. I continue to let Him know how I feel, what I think, and why I think the way I do. Wounds and lies still show up, but I continue to develop a firsthand knowledge of Father God, Jesus, and the Holy Spirit.

As far as I am along the road to healing, I still, like everyone else, have issues in my life. Sometimes I struggle to feel safe. Other times, I don't feel valued as a person. I experience times when I look at the Holy Spirit and don't have a clue what to do or say. Each of these obstacles has changed in how they present themselves over the years, but I deal with them much differently now—probably better because I have improved through years of hard work. I allow the Godhead to be part of how I process life because I have developed an honest relationship through transparency and openness.

Over the years, I have come to realize that possessing firsthand knowledge of God is an effective answer to many problems. So many people think answers come from changing their pasts or situations. I used to believe that too. Life and my perceptions of God have taught me otherwise; we cannot change our pasts or most of our circumstances.

When the Godhead partners with us in those situations we want to change, we handle people and situations quite differently. Situations may or may not change immediately, but having firsthand knowledge of the Lord allows us to navigate hard times and to not crash-and-burn or be upset if things don't change.

Even when I feel like I have messed up or not handled situations correctly, I look to Father God and wait for His response. Typically, He looks at me and says, "You're okay." Then Holy Spirit hugs me and says, "You're fine." Meanwhile, Jesus stands there and gives me a friendly thumbs-up.

Most of the people who come to my office don't come thinking that having firsthand knowledge of God can be the answer that will actually solve their problems. They think the answer is in changing their situations or the people around them. Their pasts cannot be altered, but something has to improve.

For Job and I, the first step was to be willing to take a risk in pursuing an interaction with the Lord, even if we were afraid of what He might do or say. Job faced this when God appeared in the midst of a storm, *"finally, God answered Job from the eye of a violent storm"* (Job 38:1). I imagine the storm would have been a scary place for Job, not knowing what was going to happen next.

For me, the first real risk was when I was "beating up Father God." That was a scary place for me. It was risky because I didn't know what He would do. Was He going to punish me? Beat me up? Or cast me out? What He did do was kiss my face all over. You have to risk not getting your questions answered to get what He wants to give you. You don't have to accept or believe any information He offers. You will be the one who is in charge of what to believe and how to apply it.

If you are willing to go on this journey, then I encourage you to take the first step. Take some time to sense or feel where Father God is. Try to sense or get an impression of where He might be. He may seem distant or close. If He appears far away, that is fine. If He seems too close, ask Him to move back to a location that feels safe.

Never assume what Father God will do or say. You may not hear words or see a picture. Remember, my goal at this point is for you just to gain information about Father God's viewpoint. The aim is not to find out what actions you need to take to be fixed. All you need right now is information.

Once you have a sense or impression of Him, ask, "Father God, are You mad or disappointed with me? Do You aim to punish me? Does Your opinion match what other people—family or friends—are saying to me?"

You have now started the journey of connecting with God for that firsthand knowledge. In Job's case, God did not agree with any of the information his friends gave and maybe that will be the same for you.

The next step is to find out what information the Lord wants you to know. The first question can be, "Father God, what do You think or feel about me?"

His answer will be different for each person. Some people will hear words; others will sense His pleasure. Some will experience peace—others an impression of love. Some will see a picture of Him holding their hands; others will catch a glimpse Him standing on a mountain proclaiming His love.

Give yourself permission to receive His insights, and don't succumb to the fear of having to apply them right away. For me, it wasn't an overnight process to learn the truths God revealed.

The third step is to ask, "Father God, why do you think or feel that way? Whatever answers He provides, take time to decide what you will do with that information. Will you receive it, accept it, and apply it to your life? When you are in difficult situations, will you remember what the Godhead has told you and apply its wisdom?

Remember when the woman at the training session shared her frustrations with me? I had a choice whether to believe the information Father God gave me or to continue being mad and upset. I had to make a decision no matter what—even if things didn't go my way after I applied it. Will you go to Father God and let Him know what you are feeling and thinking?

We all, as humans, have needs that need to be met, even as Christians. The members of the Godhead would like to meet them for you. When others around you are unable or unwilling to meet your needs, this connection with the Godhead can provide firsthand knowledge that can bring healing.

Go out and start the journey. Live your life. Don't be afraid of the people and the situations you meet. It's all an opportunity to start developing that connection with God that leads to in-depth knowledge.

For me, this has been an amazing journey. After reading Job and hearing what the friends had to say, and discovering how God responded, and then seeing Job's reaction to all this information, I asked myself, "Do I have an honest relationship with the Lord? Do I have firsthand knowledge of Him?"

I realized I wasn't always being honest and that I too lived on crumbs and rumors. This started me on a path toward discovering an in-depth knowledge of the Lord— and the only way I or any person can do that is to live life. So, go now and live a full life.

GLOSSARY

Almighty God: appears in the prologue, climax, and epilogue sections of the story. When He appears at the end of Elihu's speech, He doesn't address any of Job's circumstances. He instead asks Job who he is and where he was during the time of creation. His questions ultimately lead Job to repentance.

Bildad the Shuhite: one of Job's friends. He tries to convince Job of his sin and reaffirms Eliphaz's statements that God is all-powerful and rules over everything.

Elihu: appears late in the story and tries to correct everyone's viewpoint of God. Elihu does a good job listing and arguing God's attitudes, but like the others, does not take much time to hear Job's point of view. Some scholars speculate Elihu to be the potential author of the book.

Elihu's Speeches: the section of the story that involves Elihu's arguments. Because Elihu has no proper introduction or exit, some scholars believe him to be a later addition.

Eliphaz the Termanite: the first of Job's friends to speak. He spends the majority of his time trying to convince Job of his sin and affirms God's power and sovereignty.

Epilogue: the final section where Job is restored. He receives double of everything he had before and lives to be an old man full of years.

Job: the main character of the story who undergoes an immense transformation. Realizes by the end that his preconceived notions of God are ill-educated and repents to living on "bread crumbs of hearsay and rumor."

Nature Poems: the section where God speaks. By using the vastness of His sovereignty and nature, God questions Job's right to accuse Him of wrongdoing. If Job can't even understand the natural world, how can he expect to handle God?

Prologue: where the story begins. We meet God and satan in heaven where the challenge begins. It sets us up for the tragedies to come.

Satan: Job's accuser. He tries to trick God into harming Job by challenging his faithfulness.

Symposium: the bulk of the story that includes Job's and his friends' interactions. Their questions discuss the nature of God and the existence of evil. The bulk of it is theology and philosophy.

Trey: a fictional character created for the purposes of this book to place readers in the heart of Job's world.

Zophar the Naamathite: another of Job's friends. He confirms what Eliphaz says and adds too that God is all-powerful. Like his other two friends, Zophar is set on showing Job the "right way."

ABOUT TERESA LIEBSCHER

TERESA LIEBSCHER IS A CO-LEADER OF THE Bethel Sozo ministry headquarters at Bethel Church in Redding, CA. She is also the founder and leader of the Shabar ministry. Teresa travels the world training, mentoring and ministering in both Bethel Sozo and the Shabar ministries. Her passion in ministry is to help people build a healthy, relational connection with each member of the Trinity.

DESTINY IMAGE BOOKS BY
TERESA LIEBSCHER

Sozo